Essential Maths 8H

Homework Book

Elmwood Press

First published 2009 by
Elmwood Press
80 Attimore Road
Welwyn Garden City
Herts. Al8 6LP
Tel. 01707 333232

Reprinted 2012, 2013

ISBN 9781 906 622 121

Typeset and illustrated by Domex e-Data Pvt. Ltd.
Printed and bound by Bookwell

CONTENTS

UNIT 1

1.1 Properties of numbers

1   Write down all the prime numbers between 10 and 20.

2   Find all the factors of

      (a) 25   (b) 40   (c) 64

3   'The sum of all the prime numbers less than 8 is 17'. True or false?

4   (a) List all the factors of 30.

      (b) List all the factors of 48.

      (c) Write down the highest common factor of 30 and 48.

5   Find the highest common factor of 32 and 80.

6   Which numbers below are prime?

$$39 \qquad 43 \qquad 31 \qquad 49 \qquad 51$$

7   Three factors of 20 add up to 16. Write down two different ways in which this can be done.

8   Answer true or false:
      'All square numbers have exactly 3 factors.'

1   Add together all the prime numbers between 20 and 30.

2   Which numbers below are multiples of 7?

$$35 \qquad 77 \qquad 21 \qquad 39 \qquad 51 \qquad 42$$

3   (a) Write down the first six multiples of 15.

      (b) Write down the first six multiples of 20.

      (c) Write down the lowest common multiple (LCM) of 15 and 20.

4   Find the LCM of

      (a) 12 and 18   (b) 10 and 16   (c) 9 and 6

2

5 Why can a prime number not have 0 as its last digit?

6 Copy and fill in the empty boxes for this sequence.

| 1 | 3 | 6 | 10 | | 21 | | | 45 |

7 A baker's van delivers to a village every 5 days. A butcher's van delivers every 7 days. How often will the baker and butcher deliver on the same day?

8 The number p is a multiple of 8 between 50 and 60. The number q is a multiple of 12 between 20 and 30. Work out $p - q$.

9 Answer true or false: 'A square number always has an odd number of factors.' *Explain* your answer.

10 Write the number 84 as the sum of four square numbers.

HWK 2M ——————————————————————— **Main Book Page 5**

1 Copy and complete this factor tree.

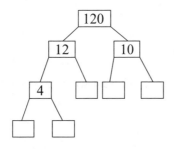

$$120 = \boxed{} \times \boxed{} \times \boxed{} \times \boxed{} \times \boxed{}$$

2 Draw factor trees for the following numbers.

(a) 50   (b) 240   (c) 420   (d) 1820   (e) 1617

3 $\boxed{105 = 3 \times 5 \times 7}$ and $\boxed{110 = 2 \times 5 \times 11}$

Find the highest common factor of 105 and 110.

4 $\boxed{210 = 2 \times 3 \times 5 \times 7}$ and $\boxed{525 = 3 \times 5 \times 5 \times 7}$

Find the highest common factor of 210 and 525.

5 (a) Draw a factor tree for 630.

(b) Draw a factor tree for 1560.

(c) Use your answers to find the highest common factor of 630 and 1560.

6 (a) Given $196 = 2 \times 2 \times 7 \times 7$, find $\sqrt{196}$

(b) Given $9801 = 3 \times 3 \times 3 \times 3 \times 11 \times 11$, find $\sqrt{9801}$

7 Write 1764 as the product of its prime factors and then find $\sqrt{1764}$.

HWK 2E   **Main Book Page 6**

1 Work out

(a) 2^3 (b) 8^3 (c) 20^3 (d) $\sqrt[3]{1}$ (e) $\sqrt[3]{216}$

2 Which is larger? 4^5 or 5^4

3 Write down which calculations below give an answer greater than 200.

(a) $5^3 + 4^2$ (b) $3^4 + 6^3$ (c) $2^8 - 1^7$ (d) $10^3 - 9^3$

4 Work out, without a calculator.

(a) 12^2 (b) $\left(\frac{1}{4}\right)^2$ (c) 10^4 (d) 0.4^2 (e) 0.1^3

5 '5 to the power of 5 is 3125'. True or false?

6 Use the $\boxed{x^y}$ key (or $\boxed{y^x}$) on a calculator to work out

(a) 4^6 (b) 0.7^4 (c) 3^8 (d) 3.2^5 (e) 0.1^6

7 Find values of a and b such that

$$a^2 + 44 = b^3$$

8 Copy and complete the following:

(a) If $m = 3^2$ and $n = 3^5$, then $mn = 3^\square$

(b) If $x = 7^2$ and $y = 7^4$, then $xy = 7^\square$

9 Find values of p and q such that

$$p^3 + 57 = q^2$$

10 Maurice says that '$4^3 \times 4^3 = 4^6$' and Sarah says that '$4^3 \times 4^3 = 4^9$'. Who is correct? *Justify* your answer.

1.2 Fractions

1   Cancel down each fraction to its simplest terms:

(a) $\dfrac{9}{39}$ (b) $\dfrac{16}{40}$ (c) $\dfrac{36}{60}$ (d) $\dfrac{50}{125}$ (e) $\dfrac{40}{500}$

2   Which fraction is *not* equivalent to the others?

$\left(\dfrac{12}{15}\right)$ $\left(\dfrac{20}{25}\right)$ $\left(\dfrac{8}{10}\right)$ $\left(\dfrac{32}{40}\right)$ $\left(\dfrac{25}{30}\right)$ $\left(\dfrac{24}{30}\right)$

3   Change these improper fractions to mixed numbers.

(a) $\dfrac{11}{6}$ (b) $\dfrac{33}{10}$ (c) $\dfrac{21}{8}$ (d) $\dfrac{15}{7}$ (e) $\dfrac{29}{5}$

4   Change these mixed numbers to improper fractions.

(a) $5\frac{3}{8}$ (b) $2\frac{7}{9}$ (c) $6\frac{1}{6}$ (d) $4\frac{2}{5}$ (e) $5\frac{7}{10}$

5   Answer true or false:

(a) $\dfrac{18}{24}=\dfrac{3}{4}$ (b) $\dfrac{7}{8}=\dfrac{24}{32}$ (c) $\dfrac{5}{9}=\dfrac{20}{36}$ (d) $\dfrac{24}{28}=\dfrac{6}{7}$ (e) $\dfrac{30}{42}=\dfrac{4}{7}$ (f) $\dfrac{3}{10}=\dfrac{21}{70}$

6   Match up the improper fractions to the mixed numbers (beware: there is one odd one out).

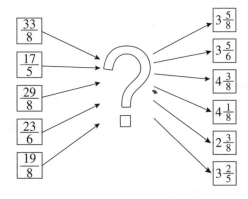

1   Copy and complete

(a) $\dfrac{3}{4}-\dfrac{1}{8}$

$=\dfrac{\square}{8}-\dfrac{1}{8}$

$=\dfrac{\square}{8}$

(b) $\dfrac{1}{3}+\dfrac{2}{15}$

$=\dfrac{\square}{15}+\dfrac{2}{15}$

$=\dfrac{\square}{15}$

(c) $\dfrac{11}{20}-\dfrac{1}{4}$

$=\dfrac{11}{20}-\dfrac{\square}{20}$

$=\dfrac{\square}{20}=\dfrac{\square}{10}$

2 Work out

(a) $\dfrac{1}{8} + \dfrac{3}{16}$ (b) $\dfrac{9}{20} - \dfrac{1}{4}$ (c) $\dfrac{11}{30} - \dfrac{1}{6}$ (d) $\dfrac{1}{12} + \dfrac{2}{3}$ (e) $\dfrac{5}{21} - \dfrac{1}{7}$ (f) $\dfrac{23}{40} - \dfrac{2}{5}$

3 Ben carpets $\dfrac{5}{8}$ of his new house. He uses wood flooring for $\dfrac{1}{4}$ of the house. The remaining floor area in his house is tiled. What fraction of the floor area is tiled?

4 Work out

(a) $\dfrac{3}{5} - \dfrac{1}{3}$ (b) $\dfrac{1}{4} + \dfrac{2}{3}$ (c) $\dfrac{2}{5} + \dfrac{3}{8}$ (d) $\dfrac{5}{7} - \dfrac{1}{8}$

(e) $\dfrac{1}{2} - \dfrac{3}{7}$ (f) $\dfrac{2}{9} + \dfrac{3}{10}$ (g) $\dfrac{7}{8} - \dfrac{2}{3}$ (h) $\dfrac{9}{10} - \dfrac{5}{7}$

5 Louise and Jake are sharing a pizza. Louise eats $\dfrac{2}{5}$ of the pizza and Jake eats $\dfrac{3}{7}$ of the pizza. What fraction of the pizza is left?

6 A test has 4 parts. This chart shows what fraction of the test each part is.

(a) What fraction of the test is part D?

(b) Janice has completed parts A and B. What fraction of the test has she still got to do?

Part A	Part B	Part C	Part D
$\dfrac{1}{3}$	$\dfrac{1}{5}$	$\dfrac{1}{4}$	?

HWK 2M   **Main Book Page 11**

1 Which answer is the odd one out?

A $\boxed{\dfrac{5}{8} \text{ of } 56}$ B $\boxed{\dfrac{4}{5} \text{ of } 45}$ C $\boxed{\dfrac{5}{6} \text{ of } 42}$

2 Martin has to travel 16 km back to his village. He runs $\dfrac{3}{8}$ of the journey then walks $\dfrac{3}{5}$ of the remaining distance. How far is he now from his village?

3 Copy and fill in the empty boxes.

(a) $\dfrac{\Box}{3}$ of $15 = 10$ (b) $\dfrac{\Box}{8}$ of $24 = 21$ (c) $\dfrac{5}{\Box}$ of $18 = 15$

4 Work out

(a) $\dfrac{1}{8} \times \dfrac{4}{5}$ (b) $\dfrac{2}{3} \times \dfrac{6}{7}$ (c) $\dfrac{3}{10} \times \dfrac{5}{6}$ (d) $\dfrac{5}{7} \times \dfrac{1}{10}$

(e) $\dfrac{4}{7} \times \dfrac{7}{8}$ (f) $\dfrac{9}{10} \times \dfrac{5}{12}$ (g) $\dfrac{5}{9} \times \dfrac{6}{7}$ (h) $\dfrac{7}{12} \times \dfrac{6}{11}$

5

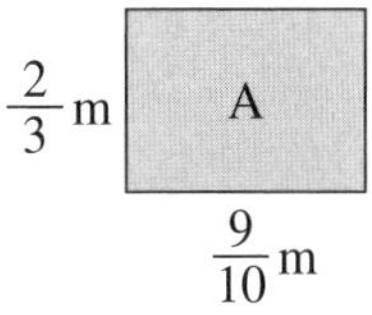

$\dfrac{2}{3}$ m   A

$\dfrac{9}{10}$ m

Which rectangle has the larger area and by how much?

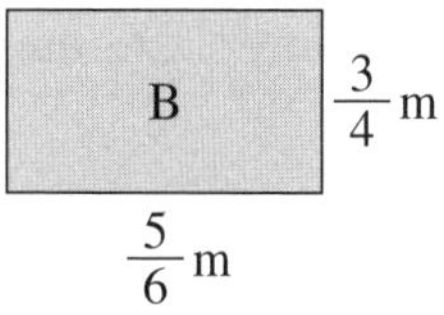

B $\dfrac{3}{4}$ m

$\dfrac{5}{6}$ m

6 Answer true or false:

(a) $\frac{3}{8} \times 4 = \frac{12}{32}$ (b) $\frac{2}{3} \times 6 = 4$ (c) $\frac{1}{6} \times 4 = \frac{2}{3}$ (d) $\frac{3}{4} \times 2 = \frac{6}{8}$

HWK 2E   **Main Book Page 12**

1 Work out, leaving each answer as a mixed number.

(a) $1\frac{1}{4} + 1\frac{1}{3}$ (b) $3\frac{1}{2} + 2\frac{1}{3}$ (c) $4\frac{3}{4} - 3\frac{1}{3}$ (d) $2\frac{1}{3} - \frac{5}{8}$ (e) $1\frac{1}{3} + 2\frac{5}{6}$ (f) $4\frac{1}{2} - 2\frac{7}{8}$

2 Copy and complete the addition square.

+	$\frac{1}{3}$			
$\frac{1}{4}$	$\frac{5}{8}$			
		$\frac{51}{70}$		
			$\frac{28}{45}$	
$\frac{2}{5}$				
	$\frac{13}{24}$	$\frac{7}{15}$		

3 Work out

(a) $\frac{5}{8} \times 20$ (b) $\frac{1}{6}$ of 15   (c) $\frac{5}{12}$ of 30   (d) $2\frac{1}{3} \times \frac{1}{2}$ (e) $3\frac{1}{2} \times 1\frac{1}{4}$ (f) $2\frac{3}{4} \times 2\frac{3}{4}$

4

not drawn to scale

Work out the total area of this shape.

5 Ahmed is given some money by his grandfather. He puts 45% of the money in the bank and spends $\frac{2}{5}$ of the money on clothes. He now has £60 of this money left in his wallet. How much money did his grandfather give him?

HWK 3M   **Main Book Page 15**

1 (a) How many fifths are there in 4?

(b) How many thirds are there in 7?

(c) How many sixths are there in 8?

2 Work out

(a) $6 \div \frac{1}{4}$ (b) $9 \div \frac{1}{7}$ (c) $3 \div \frac{1}{10}$ (d) $4 \div \frac{1}{9}$ (e) $10 \div \frac{1}{20}$ (f) $8 \div \frac{1}{50}$

3 Copy and complete each number chain.

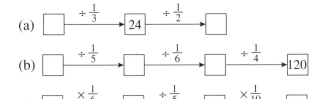

(a) ☐ $\xrightarrow{\div \frac{1}{3}}$ 24 $\xrightarrow{\div \frac{1}{2}}$ ☐

(b) ☐ $\xrightarrow{\div \frac{1}{5}}$ ☐ $\xrightarrow{\div \frac{1}{6}}$ ☐ $\xrightarrow{\div \frac{1}{4}}$ 120

(c) ☐ $\xrightarrow{\times \frac{1}{6}}$ ☐ $\xrightarrow{\div \frac{1}{5}}$ ☐ $\xrightarrow{\times \frac{1}{10}}$ 4

4 Work out $3 \div \frac{1}{5} \div \frac{1}{3}$

HWK 3E ———————————————————— **Main Book Page 16**

1 Work out

(a) $\frac{1}{4} \div \frac{1}{3}$ (b) $\frac{1}{2} \div \frac{3}{4}$ (c) $\frac{3}{8} \div \frac{1}{2}$ (d) $\frac{2}{5} \div \frac{7}{10}$

(e) $\frac{3}{5} \div \frac{7}{8}$ (f) $\frac{1}{9} \div \frac{2}{3}$ (g) $\frac{4}{7} \div \frac{7}{8}$ (h) $\frac{7}{12} \div \frac{3}{4}$

2 A strip of wood is $\frac{8}{9}$ m long. What is the total length of 12 strips of wood?

3 $\frac{1}{6}$ kg of flour is used to bake a cake. How much flour would be needed to bake 15 cakes?

4 Sam is watching his weight. He allows himself $\frac{3}{40}$ of a box of cereal for his breakfast which he measures out carefully. How many breakfasts will he get from six boxes of cereal?

5 Work out this mixture of questions.

(a) $\frac{4}{9} \div \frac{3}{5}$ (b) $\frac{1}{3} + \frac{2}{7}$ (c) $\frac{1}{4} \div \frac{5}{6}$ (d) $\frac{3}{8} \times \frac{2}{5}$

(e) $\frac{5}{8} - \frac{2}{7}$ (f) $\frac{7}{10} \times \frac{4}{5}$ (g) $\frac{3}{7} \div \frac{2}{3}$ (h) $\frac{5}{6} - \frac{3}{20}$

1.3 Area and Perimeter

HWK 1M ———————————————————— **Main Book Page 17**

1

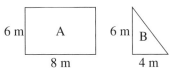

(a) Find the area of shape A.

(b) Find the area of shape B.

(c) Find the total area of both shape A and shape B.

(d) Find the area of this shape.

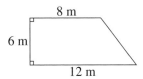

2 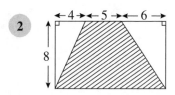 Calculate the shaded area.
(all lengths are in cm)

3 Work out the perimeter of a regular pentagon of side 7 cm.

4 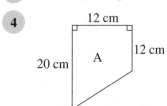 Which shape has the larger area and by how much?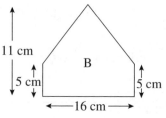

5 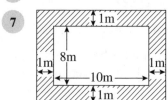 These two shapes have the same area. Find the length of the side marked x.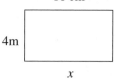

6 Work out the area of a square of perimeter 36 cm.

7 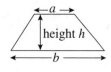 Find the area of this shaded path.

8 Draw any shape with an area of 5 cm² and perimeter 12 cm.

| HWK 1E | Main Book Page 19 |

Remember: area of parallelogram = base × height

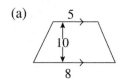 area of trapezium = $\frac{1}{2} h (a + b)$

1 Calculate the area of each shape. The lengths are in cm.

(a)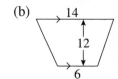

(b)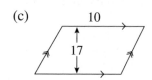

(c)

(d)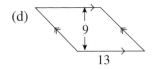

(e)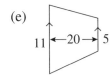

(f)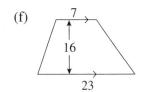

2 Calculate the value of *x* in each parallelogram below.

(a)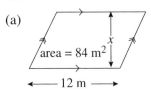

(b)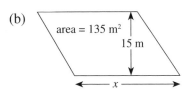

3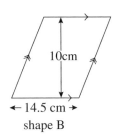

Which shape has the larger area and by how much?

shape A

shape B

4 How many square millimetres are there in one square centimetre? (Draw one square centimetre and divide it into square millimetres to check your answer)

5 How many square centimetres are there in three square metres?

HWK 2M ─────────────────────────── **Main Book Page 20**

1 Find the area of this shape.

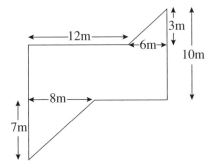

2

square A

Square A has a perimeter of 24 cm. Rectangle B has the same area as square A. Calculate the value of *x* shown on the diagram.

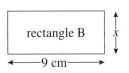

rectangle B

10

3 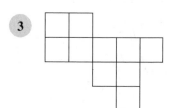 This shape, which is made using squares, has an area of 160 cm².
Find the perimeter of this shape.

4 area = 54 cm² The length of this rectangle is 3 cm greater than its width. Find the perimeter of this rectangle.

5 A triangular field has a base of $\frac{1}{2}$ km and a height of 300 m. Calculate the area of the field in hectares. (1 hectare = 10 000 m²)

6 Square A has perimeter 20 cm. Square B has perimeter 28 cm. Rectangle C has length 14 cm and width 5 cm. The area of square P is equal to the sum of the areas of square A, square B and rectangle C. Find the perimeter of square P.

7 Ashley has to paint one side of his house.
Each pot of paint covers 20 m².
How many pots of paint will Ashley
need to buy to do the job?

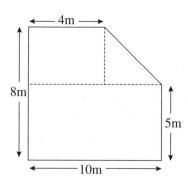

8 Draw any shape with an area of 24 cm² and perimeter 24 cm.

HWK 2E ————————————————————— **Main Book Page 21**

1 Alice wishes to carpet this room.

(a) What is the area of the room?

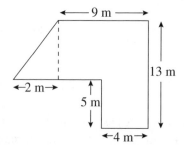

(b) 'Texas Twist' carpet costs £15.85 per square metre. 'Winchester Croft' carpet costs £17.25 per square metre. Alice decides to either carpet the whole room with 'Texas Twist' or to use 'Winchester Croft' for the L-shaped part only (so she does not carpet the triangular part of the room). Which is the cheaper option and by how much?

2 Calculate the area of each shaded shape. Give your answers in square units.

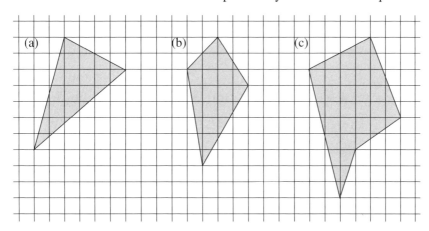

3 Jed is putting tiles onto a rectangular wall which measures 3 m by 5 m. Each tile is a square with side 10 cm. A box of 25 tiles costs £9.85.

(a) How many tiles does Jed need?

(b) How much will Jed have to pay for the tiles?

(c) Jed ends up breaking 5% of the tiles. How much *extra* must he spend on the tiles to finish the job?

4

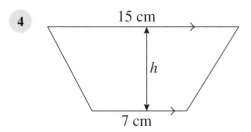

The area of this trapezium is 132 cm². Find the value of h.

5

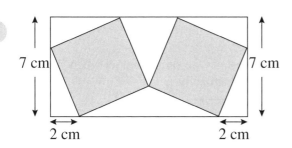

The diagram shows two squares inside a rectangle. Calculate the total area of the two grey squares.

12

1.4 Negative numbers

1 Work out

(a) $8 - (+3)$ (b) $6 + (-5)$ (c) $1 + (-3)$ (d) $5 - (-4)$

(e) $4 - (-1)$ (f) $7 + (-6)$ (g) $-3 - (-2)$ (h) $-2 + (-4)$

2 What is the difference between -19 and 17?

3 Write down the next three numbers in this sequence.

$12, 5, -2, \square, \square, \square$

4 What is the sum of $-6, 9, -8$ and -15?

5 Copy and complete this number chain.

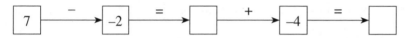

$\boxed{7} \xrightarrow{\;-\;} \boxed{-2} \xrightarrow{\;=\;} \boxed{} \xrightarrow{\;+\;} \boxed{-4} \xrightarrow{\;=\;} \boxed{}$

6 Work out

(a) $13 - (+18)$ (b) $27 + (-16)$ (c) $-14 - (-30)$ (d) $43 - (+60)$

(e) $-32 + 24$ (f) $-29 + (-12)$ (g) $53 - (-19)$ (h) $-16 - (+35)$

7 Copy and fill in the missing numbers.

(a) $-2 - \square = 1$ (b) $5 - \square = 6$ (c) $-3 + \square = -7$

8 Which calculation below gives the odd answer out?

A $\boxed{-4 + (-1)}$ B $\boxed{-3 - (-1)}$ C $\boxed{3 + (-5)}$

9 Helen has four cards as shown below.

-32 $\boxed{-18}$ + $\boxed{-14}$ + $\boxed{23}$ -9 $\boxed{-2}$ $-11 - 4$

She needs to choose one more card which will make the total of all 5 cards equal to -15.
Draw the card she needs.

10 Copy and complete these magic squares. (you must get the same number when you add across each row, add down each column and add diagonally.)

(a)

-2	-3	
	-1	
	1	

(b)

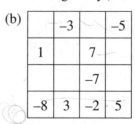

	-3		-5
1		7	
		-7	
-8	3	-2	5

1   Work out

(a) $4 \times (-3)$ (b) $-2 \times (-6)$ (c) $8 \div (-2)$ (d) $-8 \times (-3)$

(e) $-20 \div (-5)$ (f) $-28 \div (-7)$ (g) -7×2 (h) $-5 \times (-2)$

(i) $2 \times (-9)$ (j) $40 \div (-5)$ (k) $-32 \div 8$ (l) $-45 \div (-9)$

(m) $6 \times (-6)$ (n) $56 \div (-8)$ (o) $-4 \times (-1)$ (p) $-16 \div 8$

2   The temperature in Glasgow is $-4°C$. The temperature in Toronto is six times as cold. What is the temperature in Toronto?

3   Which question below gives the highest answer and by how much?

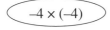 $-4 \times (-4)$ 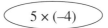 $5 \times (-4)$

4 -32 is divided by each number below. Write down which of these numbers will give an answer greater than zero.

| 4 | | −8 | | −2 | | 16 | | 32 |

5   Answer true or false.

(a) $-3 \times (-3) = -9$ (b) $(-3)^2 = 9$ (c) $-5 \times (-4) = 20$

(d) $2 \times (-3) \times (-4) = 24$ (e) $(-5)^2 = 10$ (f) $-1 \times (-1) \times (-1) = -1$

6   Copy and complete this number chain.

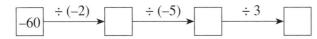

$$-60 \xrightarrow{\div (-2)} \square \xrightarrow{\div (-5)} \square \xrightarrow{\div 3} \square$$

7   Work out

(a) $(-6)^2 \div (-3)$ (b) $0 \times (-4)$ (c) $(-2)^2 \times (-3)^2$

(d) $(-8) \times 4 \times (-5)$ (e) $(-4)^3 \times 2$ (f) $(-2)^3 \div (-4)$

1   Work out

(a) $-9 + 7$ (b) $-3 - (-2)$ (c) $-10 - (+4)$ (d) $5 \times (-9)$

(e) $-16 \div 8$ (f) $-28 \div (-4)$ (g) $13 - 40$ (h) $7 \times (-3)$

(i) $(-9)^2$ (j) $-8 + (-2)$ (k) $-36 \div (-12)$ (l) $23 - (-9)$

2 Copy and complete this number chain.

$$3 \xrightarrow{\times (-3)} \square \xrightarrow{\times 2} \square \xrightarrow{\times (-5)^2} \square$$

3 Copy and complete these calculations.

(a) $-6 \times \square = -30$ (b) $9 \times \square = -36$ (c) $-10 \times \square = 70$

(d) $\square \times (-2) = -14$ (e) $-8 \times \square = 32$ (f) $\square \times (-8) = 48$

4 Find the values of x and y if

$$x + y = 2 \quad \text{and} \quad xy = -8$$

5 Find the values of p and q if

$$p + q = -2 \quad \text{and} \quad pq = -15$$

6 Copy and complete this multiplication table.

×	−5		
		−9	6
4			−8
	35		

7 (a) Find two numbers whose sum is −3 and whose product is −18. ('product' means multiplied together)

(b) Find two numbers whose sum is −5 and whose product is 6.

(c) Find two numbers whose sum is −9 and whose product is 20.

1.5 Sequences

HWK 1M ——————————————————————— **Main Book Page 33**

1 (a) 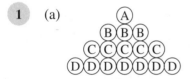 Draw the next row which will fit onto the bottom of this triangle.

(b) How many circles are used in total for the triangle in part (a) if seven rows are drawn?

2 Write down each sequence and find the missing numbers

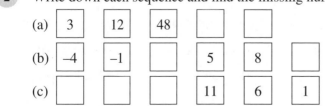

(a) | 3 | 12 | 48 | | |

(b) | −4 | −1 | | 5 | 8 | |

(c) | | | | 11 | 6 | 1 |

3 Find the next term in each sequence.

(a) 1, 1, 2, 3, 5, 8, ...

(b) 26, 24, 21, 17, ...

(c) $\dfrac{5}{8}, \dfrac{10}{16}, \dfrac{15}{24}, \dfrac{20}{32}, \ldots$

(d) −9, −16, −23, −30, ...

(e) $2n, 5n, 8n, 11n, \ldots$

(f) $\dfrac{1}{2}, 0.55, \dfrac{3}{5}, 0.65, \ldots$

4 Luke says the next number in the sequence 1 2 4 is 8 . Ali says that he is wrong and the next number is 7 . Tom says that they are both correct. *Explain* why.

5 Find the next two terms in each sequence.

(a) 121, 144, 169, 196, ...

(b) 360, 180, 60, 15, ...

(c) 1, 8, 27, 64, ...

HWK 1E ———————————————————— **Main Book Page 34**

1 The first term of a sequence is 4. Write down the first four terms of the sequence if the rule is:

(a) multiply by 3 and add 1

(b) double and add 4

2 Find the rule for each sequence. Each rule has two operations (similar to the rules in question (**1**) above).

(a) 3 ⟶ 9 ⟶ 21 ⟶ 45

(b) 1 ⟶ 3 ⟶ 11 ⟶ 43

(c) 1 ⟶ 6 ⟶ 31 ⟶ 156

3 Find the missing numbers in these linear sequences.

(a) | 6 | | 14 | 18 | | |

(b) | | 23 | 16 | | 2 | |

(c) | | 49 | | | | 17 |

4 A linear sequence has a 3rd term of 15 and a 4th term of 19. What is the 2nd term?

5 A linear sequence has a 1st term of 7 and a 3rd term of 19. What is the 4th term?

6 The rule for this sequence is 'multiply by 2 and add 2'. Find the missing numbers.

◯ ⟶ ⑩ ⟶ ㉒ ⟶ ◯

7 Write down the rule for this sequence.

② ⟶ ⑤ ⟶ ⑭ ⟶ ㊶

8 Write down the first five terms of these sequences.

(a) the second term is 9 and the rule is 'subtract 11'

(b) the fourth term is 35 and the rule is 'add 6'

(c) the first two terms are 0, 3 and the rule is 'add the two previous terms'

(d) the third term is 48 and the rule is 'divide by 4'

(e) the fourth term is –11 and the rule is 'add 9'

| HWK 2M/2E | Main Book Page 37 |

1 Here is a sequence 5 7 10 14. Write the numbers in a table as shown.

Predict the numbers shown with ? marks to find the next two terms in the sequence 5, 7, 10, 14.

terms	differences
5	
	2
7	
	3
10	
	4
14	
	?
?	
	?
?	

2 Predict the next two terms in each sequence.

(a) 3, 8, 15, 24, ...   (b) 53, 41, 31, 23, ...   (c) 80, 71, 63, 56, ...   (d) 24, 39, 57, 78, ...

3 Here is a sequence of matchstick squares.

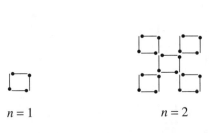 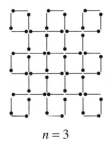

$n = 1$ $n = 2$ $n = 3$

Shape number, n	Number of matches	Difference
1	4	
		16
2	20	
		32
3	52	
		48
4	100	
5	?	

Use the differences to predict the number of matches in shape number 5.

4 This sequence is more difficult. The first differences make no obvious pattern. Work out the second differences and find the missing numbers.

Number	difference
3	
	1
4	
	4
8	
	9
17	
	16
33	

Number	difference	second difference
3		
	1	
4		3
	4	
8		5
	9	
17		7
	16	
33		(?)
	(?)	

5 Use first, second and third differences to predict the next number in each of the sequences below.

(a) 5
    7
   11
   20
   37
   (?)

(b) 7
   12
   20
   35
   61
   (?)

(c) 1
   9
   21
   46
   93
   (?)

6 Write down the first number in the sequence below which will *exceed* 1000.

4, 12, 25, 50, 94, 164, …

1.6 Using a calculator

HWK 1M ——————————————————————— **Main Book Page 43**

1 Answer true or false.

(a) $(3 + 4)^2 = 49$

(b) $8^2 - 4 = 12$

(c) $8 + 3 \times 2 = 22$

(d) $5^2 - 3^2 = 16$

(e) $19 + 3 \times 4 = 31$

(f) $4 \times (6 + 3) = 27$

(g) $(4^2 + 2^2) \div 5 = 4$

(h) $\dfrac{25 - 8 \times 2}{3} = 3$

(i) $5 + 6^2 \div 9 = 9$

In questions ② to ⑩ find the missing signs (+, −, ×, ÷). There are no brackets.

2 8 2 3 = 19

3 5 3 1 = 2

4 4 18 3 = 10

5 20 2 15 = 25

6 9 16 4 = 21

7 5 9 2 = 23

8 16 14 2 1 = 10

9 10 2 3 4 = 17

10 9 4 2 3 = 14

The next six questions have brackets.

11 4 5 2 = 12

12 8 3 4 = 44

13 8 2 4 3 = 42

14 9 4 1 7 = 10

15 15 25 7 3 = 4

16 8 5 6 20 = 18

17 Copy each question below and write brackets so that each calculation gives the correct answer.

(a) $13 + 17 \div 5 = 6$

(b) $5 + 20 \div 3 + 2 = 5$

(c) $10 - 6 \div 1 + 3 = 1$

HWK 1E   **Main Book Page 44**

Use a calculator and give answers correct to two decimal places. Remember BIDMAS.

1 $5.94^2 - 1.6$

2 $\dfrac{61}{4.7} + 3.9$

3 $5.3 + 2.9 \times 1.7$

4 $6.18 - 7 \div 13$

5 $13 \div 11 + 4.19$

6 $6.2 + \dfrac{4.3}{2.19}$

7 $8.24 + 15 \div 9.6$

8 $3.16^2 \div 27$

9 $3.51 - 2.17 \times 0.83$

10 $5.6 - \dfrac{16.4}{13}$

11 $5.12^2 \div 39$

12 $\dfrac{12.4 - 5.17}{2.3}$

13 $5.83 + 6.3 \times 2.19$

14 $\dfrac{8.3 + 16.14}{5.5}$

15 $1.739 + 4.7^2$

16 $\dfrac{2.6^2 + 1.35}{4.7}$

17 $16.14 - 0.38^2$

18 $\dfrac{(1.78 - 0.114)^2}{0.383}$

19 $6.3 \times (2.18 - 1.09)$

20 $\dfrac{1.17}{(0.68 + 0.23)^2}$

21 $\dfrac{1.16^2}{4.8^2}$

22 Jade sells security devices. She makes 8 selling trips to the north–west of England during one month. Each trip costs her £49.50. During the month she sells seven burglar alarms and 12 security spotlights. She makes £179 profit for each burglar alarm sold and £23 for each spotlight. How much money will she make in total during this month?

23 Jimmy squares the number 4.7 then adds on 28. Abbie subtracts 3.6 from 10 then cubes the answer. Calculate the product of the two final answers.

24 Calculate the following, giving your answer to two decimal places.

$$\frac{(7.8^2 + 1.9)^2 - 6.3^2}{(8.91 - 3.6)^2 + 6.4 \times 3.4}$$

HWK 2M   **Main Book Page 45**

Work out and give the answer correct to 2 decimal places.

1 $7.49 \times (8.16 - 3.64)$

2 $(1.93 + 4.78) \div 2.38$

3 $(7.49 \times 8.16) - 3.64$

4 $1.87 + \left(\dfrac{3.29}{1.6}\right)$

5 $5.65 \div (8.2 - 4.16)$

6 $\dfrac{7.92}{(1.82 + 3.03)}$

7 $\dfrac{(9.23 - 2.14)}{6.49}$

8 $0.18^2 \times 2.3$

9 $8.36 + 3.7^2$

10 $(3.62 + 2.59)^2$

11 $(7.12 + 4.93 - 1.86)^2 \times 1.6$

12 $\left(\dfrac{5.6}{1.93}\right) + 4.18$

13 $\dfrac{(11.6 - 3.14)}{(2.12 + 5.9)}$

14 $0.93^2 + 0.26^2$

15 $(5.1 \times 2.48) + (3.6 \times 2.9)$

16 $\dfrac{7.94}{2.16^2}$

17 $(8.29 - 2.11)^2$

18 $\dfrac{1.93^2}{(5.06 - 2.1)}$

19 $(7.62^2 \times 4.9) - 1.6^2$

20 $\dfrac{(8.62 + 3.59)}{(21.4 - 6.28)}$

HWK 3M ———————————————————— **Main Book Page 46**

Work out, using a calculator ($a\frac{b}{c}$ button)

1 $\dfrac{5}{7} - \dfrac{1}{5}$

2 $\dfrac{3}{4} \times \dfrac{7}{8}$

3 $\dfrac{1}{6} + \dfrac{3}{11}$

4 $\dfrac{6}{7} - \dfrac{3}{5}$

5 $\dfrac{4}{9} + \dfrac{3}{10}$

6 $\dfrac{7}{10} + \dfrac{7}{8}$

7 $3\dfrac{1}{4} - \dfrac{2}{3}$

8 $2\dfrac{1}{2} + 1\dfrac{3}{5}$

9 $3\dfrac{1}{3} - 1\dfrac{1}{2}$

10 $2\dfrac{3}{4} \times 1\dfrac{5}{6}$

11 $4\dfrac{2}{5} \div 1\dfrac{1}{4}$

12 $6\dfrac{1}{2} \div 2\dfrac{1}{6}$

13 Alana watches two films, one after the other. The first film lasts $1\dfrac{2}{3}$ hours and the second film lasts $2\dfrac{1}{10}$ hours. What is the total running time of both films?

14 A piece of timber is $3\dfrac{1}{4}$ m long. Terry uses two-thirds of the piece of timber. What length of timber does Terry use?

15 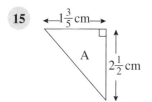 Which shape has the larger area and by how much?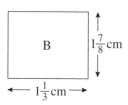

16 Work out

(a) $\dfrac{7}{10} + \dfrac{2}{3} \times \dfrac{5}{6}$

(b) $\dfrac{9}{11} - 1\dfrac{1}{10} \div 4\dfrac{1}{2}$

(c) $3\dfrac{1}{4} \times 1\dfrac{1}{3} - 2\dfrac{3}{5}$

17 Copy and complete.

(a) $3\dfrac{1}{3} + \boxed{} = 5\dfrac{1}{4}$

(b) $\boxed{} \div \dfrac{4}{5} = 3\dfrac{1}{3}$

(c) $\boxed{} \times 2\dfrac{2}{3} = 9\dfrac{11}{21}$

HWK 3E ———————————————————— **Main Book Page 46**

Work out, using a calculator ($a\frac{b}{c}$ button)

1 $\dfrac{2}{3} \times \left(\dfrac{3}{4} - \dfrac{1}{5}\right)$

2 $\dfrac{9}{10} \div \left(\dfrac{3}{5} - \dfrac{3}{20}\right)$

3 $\left(\dfrac{4}{9} + \dfrac{2}{5}\right) \times \dfrac{3}{4}$

4 $\dfrac{5}{7} \times \left(2\dfrac{1}{4} - \dfrac{7}{8}\right)$

5 $\left(3\dfrac{1}{2}\right)^2 + \dfrac{5}{6}$

6 $4\dfrac{1}{4} \div 1\dfrac{1}{2} + \dfrac{5}{9}$

7 $\dfrac{2}{7} \times \dfrac{4}{5} + \dfrac{3}{8} \times \dfrac{2}{3}$

8 $\left(\dfrac{5}{8} - \dfrac{1}{3}\right)^2$

9 $\dfrac{\left(2\frac{1}{2} + 3\frac{2}{5}\right)}{\left(1\frac{1}{5} - \frac{5}{6}\right)}$

10 Copy and complete this multiplication table.

×		$\frac{1}{5}$	$2\frac{1}{4}$		
$\frac{1}{2}$					
$1\frac{1}{3}$					
$\frac{7}{9}$	$\frac{14}{27}$			$\frac{35}{54}$	
	$\frac{4}{25}$				$\frac{2}{5}$
					$\frac{1}{3}$

11 Copy and complete.

(a) $\dfrac{4}{5} \times \left(\dfrac{3}{4} - \square\right) = \dfrac{1}{15}$

(b) $\left(2\frac{1}{3} + \square\right) \times \left(3\frac{1}{2} - 2\frac{7}{8}\right) = 1\frac{53}{72}$

(c) $\left(3\frac{1}{4}\right)^2 - 2\frac{3}{4} \times \square = 6\frac{7}{16}$

(d) $\left(1\frac{2}{3} \div \dfrac{3}{5} + \square\right) \times \left(\dfrac{1}{2}\right)^3 = \dfrac{73}{180}$

HWK 4M   **Main Book Page 47**

Work out the following. Give each answer correct to one decimal place where appropriate.

1 $-9 \div (-2)$

2 $-18 - 14$

3 $-6.2 \times (-3.1)$

4 $4.8 - (-3.72)$

5 $-46 \div 4.13$

6 $(-8.12)^2$

7 $\dfrac{(-7) \times 2}{-5}$

8 $9 - 4.6^2$

9 $\dfrac{8 - (-0.17)}{2.3}$

10 $\left(\dfrac{-3.6}{1.92}\right) - (-2.8)$

11 $(-7.2 - 3.93)^2$

12 $49 - (-4.6)^2$

13 Copy and complete:

(a) $-3.7 + \square = 12.1$

(b) $5.17 + \square = -11.03$

(c) $\dfrac{-12.48}{\square} = -2.6$

(d) $4.3 \times \square = -29.24$

14 Which calculation gives the larger answer and by how much?

A $\boxed{(-4.9)^2 + 4.52}$

B $\boxed{(-5.2 + 10.31)^2 - 2.06}$

15 Which calculation gives the larger answer and by how much?

A $\boxed{\sqrt{(4.1 - (-8.15))}}$

B $\boxed{\dfrac{4.16 + (-1.9)^2}{2}}$

Work out correct to 1 decimal place.

1 $1.83 + (7.2 \times 3.4) - (1.9 \times 2.6)$

2 $(5.7 \times 3.2) + 4.5^2 + 2.8^3$

3 $19.6 - (0.3 + 1.6 \times 1.8^2)$

4 $22.4 - 1.9^3$

5 $(7.3 \times 4.9) + 3.4^3 - (1.8 \times 2.6)$

6 $5.8^3 + 5.8^2 + 5.8$

7   Find the total cost of the items shown opposite, correct to the nearest penny.

> 2 packets of cream crackers at 67p per packet
> 1 jar of pickle at £1.64
> 150 g of cheese at £4.90/kg
> 4 tins of baked beans at 59 p each

8

Ron's items
2 tins of paint at £11.99 each
4 paintbrushes at £3.45 each
300 g of nails at £7/kg
12 m of wallpaper at £4.70/metre

(a) Who has the most expensive bill, Ron or Amy?

(b) What is the difference in the two bills?

Amy's items
2 paintbrushes at £4.25 each
200 g of nails at £8/kg
14m of wallpaper at £4.55/metre
3 batons of wood at £6.80 per baton

9   Give answers correct to 1 decimal place.

(a) $\dfrac{4.9}{8} + \dfrac{6.3}{17}$

(b) $\sqrt{\dfrac{80.6}{4.17 + 3.8}}$

(c) $\dfrac{385}{7.6^3 + 123}$

(d) $2.9^4 - \left(\dfrac{2.8}{3.4}\right)^2$

(e) $\dfrac{(-4.62) \times 1.8}{(-2.53)}$

(f) $\dfrac{3}{5}$ of $\left(\dfrac{4.9^2}{3.72}\right)^2$

(g) 5.4% of 6% of 1270

(h) $4.6^5 - 7.3^4$

(i) $\dfrac{7.3^2 + \sqrt{15.4}}{5.8^2 - \sqrt{98}}$

(j) $(7\% \text{ of } 48.6)^4$

(k) $\dfrac{8}{9}$ of $\left(\dfrac{5}{6} - \dfrac{2}{5}\right)^2$

(l) $\sqrt{\dfrac{\sqrt{15} - 1.8^2}{2.73^3 - \sqrt{12}}}$

UNIT 2

2.1 Written calculations

HWK 1M ———————————————————— **Main Book Page 61**

Work out, without a calculator

1 3200 − 1593	**2** 7.18 × 8	**3** 314 × 9	**4** 0.8 × 10000
5 87 × 30	**6** 22.4 ÷ 8	**7** 62 ÷ 1000	**8** 39 × 400
9 3684 + 2153	**10** 0.0654 ÷ 3	**11** 0.82 − 0.157	**12** 840 ÷ 12
13 12.74 ÷ 7	**14** 56 × 43	**15** 30 × 25	**16** 7.4 × 1000
17 928 ÷ 32	**18** 0.183 + 6 + 0.24	**19** 688 ÷ 43	**20** 42 × 300
21 429 × 67	**22** 7 − 3.014	**23** 144000 ÷ 60	**24** 429 × 73

HWK 1E ———————————————————— **Main Book Page 62**

1

packet of crisps 48p
bottle of water £1.06
currant bun 39p

Sally buys 3 packets of crisps, 2 bottles of water and 2 currant buns. How much change will she get from £10?

2 How many currant buns in question **1** could you buy with £5?

3 Which is larger and by how much?

6.2 ÷ 100   or   0.8 − 0.739

4 Colin weighs 63.64 kg and Marie weighs 51.87 kg. How much heavier is Colin?

5 Work out, without a calculator

(a) 9.3 × 4000   (b) 4.92 × 0.25   (c) 0.169 × 1000   (d) 36 + 16.2

(e) 0.82 − 0.073   (f) 0.312 ÷ 6   (g) 8.19 × 0.5   (h) 6.4 × 3000

(i) 0.019 + 3.685   (j) 6 − 0.018   (k) 0.86 × 7   (l) 0.513 ÷ 9

6 Charlie is sponsored £3.20 per kilometre for a charity run. How much money is he given if he runs 13.8 km?

7 Copy and complete.

(a) 3.9 + ☐ = 6.34   (b) 0.28 ÷ ☐ = 0.0028   (c) 9 − ☐ = 4.44

(d) ☐ − 0.19 = 0.34   (e) ☐ × 0.5 = 1.69   (f) ☐ + 2.91 = 10.15

HWK 2M ———————————————————————————— **Main Book Page 63**

For each of the scales work out the measurement shown by each arrow.

1
7   a   b   8
m

2
13   a   b   14
kg

3
60   a   b   80
m

4
0.4   a   b   0.5
cm

5
20   a   b   70
g

6
3   a   b   8
m

7
kg
6

←b

←a
2

8
litres
5

←b

←a
1

9
metres
10

←b

←a

6

10   Copy the line and locate the numbers.

| 4.02 | 3.96 | 3.92 | 4.08 | 4.06 |

3.9   4.1

11   Copy the line and locate the numbers.

| 2.35 | 2.365 | 2.38 | 2.31 | 2.325 |

2.3   2.4

12   Write down the measurement shown by each arrow below.

a   b   c   d
           4.0   4.1

HWK 2E ———————————————————————————— **Main Book Page 64**

1   Answer true or false.

(a) 0.08 > 0.6   (b) 0.74 > 0.069   (c) 0.063 > 0.261

(d) 0.19 < 0.51   (e) 0.006 > 0.0004   (f) 0.05 < 0.049

2   What has to be added or subtracted to change:

(a) 0.628 to 0.638   (b) 2.16 to 2.08   (c) 7.13 to 7.43?

3 Six sprinters in a race record the times shown opposite.

(a) Who won the race?

(b) Who had the slowest time?

(c) Who finished in third place?

(d) How much faster was Kyle than Mike?

John	11.78 secs
Kyle	11.69 secs
Mike	11.8 secs
Wesley	11.05 secs
Shane	11.1 secs
Alan	11.96 secs

4 Arrange in order of size, smallest first.

(a) 0.52, 0.518, 0.5

(b) 0.821, 0.833, 0.83

(c) 0.06, 0.1, 0.102, 0.094

(d) 0.35, 0.324, 0.346, 0.32

5 Write down the next number in this sequence.

3.03, 3.02, 3.01, 3, ?

6 Arrange in order of size, smallest first.

(a) 42 cm, 630 mm, 0.00048 km, 0.003 km, 3.4 m

(b) 0.009 km, 8.6 m, 890 cm, 0.0087 km, 8500 mm

HWK 3M/3E   **Main Book Page 65**

1 Work out

(a) 5×0.01

(b) 32×0.1

(c) 0.2×0.3

(d) 0.7×0.4

(e) 0.3×0.06

(f) 5×0.6

(g) 7×0.001

(h) 0.6×0.07

(i) 0.4×0.001

(j) 0.02×0.04

(k) 0.03×11

(l) 0.7×0.008

2 Answer true or false.

(a) $0.3^2 = 0.9$

(b) $0.1 \times 0.2 = 0.2$

(c) $0.5^2 = 0.25$

3 A four metre width of carpet costs £8.35 per metre. Calculate the cost of 6.4 m of carpet.

4

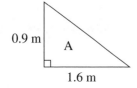

Which shape has the larger area and by how much?

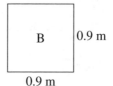

5 Copy and complete the multiplication square.

✕	0.3	0.05	7	1.2	0.9
0.6					
0.05					
1.1					
0.8					
4					

6 £1 can be changed for $1.46.

(a) How many dollars do you get for £300?

(b) How many dollars do you get for £550?

7 Copy and complete

(a) $0.4 \times \boxed{} = 0.024$　　(b) $\boxed{}^2 = 0.0025$　　(c) $\boxed{} \times 0.08 = 0.096$

HWK 4M ——————————————————————— **Main Book Page 67**

Work out an approximate answer to each question below first and then find the accurate answer *without* using a calculator. Look at your approximate answer to check if your accurate answer seems reasonable.

1 5.3×4.9　　**2** 9.7×22　　**3** 2.9×18　　**4** 68×0.31

5 19.4×3.2　　**6** 48.6×4.9　　**7** 0.419×53　　**8** 0.54×0.29

9 8.7×37.3　　**10** 0.86×62.3　　**11** 71.6×0.95　　**12** 0.342×47

13 59.9×0.012　　**14** 0.068×3.06　　**15** 83×0.0593　　**16** 6.18×0.089

HWK5M/5E ——————————————————————— **Main Book Page 67**

1 Work out

(a) $8 \div 0.1$　　(b) $43 \div 0.1$　　(c) $0.6 \div 0.1$　　(d) $7 \div 0.01$

(e) $0.2 \div 0.01$　　(f) $22 \div 0.01$　　(g) $58 \div 0.1$　　(h) $0.9 \div 0.01$

2 How many 0.1 kg amounts of sugar can be obtained from 2.4 kg of sugar?

3 Answer true or false.

(a) $0.4 \div 0.01 = 4$　　(b) $31 \div 0.1 = 310$　　(c) $45 \div 0.01 = 450$

(d) $0.8 \div 0.01 = 800$　　(e) $1 \div 0.01 = 100$　　(f) $0.9 \div 0.1 = 9$

4 Work out, without a calculator

(a) $6.39 \div 0.3$　　(b) $0.72 \div 0.4$　　(c) $0.49 \div 0.2$　　(d) $1.158 \div 0.6$

(e) $3.78 \div 0.3$ (f) $0.1174 \div 0.02$ (g) $0.01352 \div 0.08$ (h) $9.52 \div 0.7$

(i) $0.0126 \div 0.09$ (j) $0.6656 \div 0.8$ (k) $0.01528 \div 0.002$ (l) $0.0655 \div 0.005$

5  A domino is 4.8 cm long. Hundreds of dominoes are laid in a line 1680 cm long. *Exactly* how many dominoes are used?

6 Find the missing numbers

(a) $14 \div \boxed{} = 1400$ (b) $5 \div \boxed{} = 50$ (c) $0.4 \div \boxed{} = 40$

(d) $\boxed{} \div 0.1 = 600$ (e) $3.6 \div \boxed{} = 36$ (f) $8.7 \div \boxed{} = 870$

7 On average a chocolate raisin weighs 0.9 g.

How many chocolate raisins will there be in a packet which weighs 76.5 g?

8 Caroline works at a garage and is paid £8.20 per hour. Scott also works at the garage and is paid £7.50 per hour.

During one week, Caroline earns £164 and Scott earns £240. Work out the total number of hours Caroline and Scott worked for during that week.

HWK 6E	**Main Book Page 69**

Hidden words

(a) Start in the top left box.

(b) Work out the answer to the calculation in the box. *Do not use a calculator.*

(c) Find the answer in the top corner of another box.

(d) Write down the letter in that box.

(e) Repeat steps (b), (c) and (d) until you arrive back at the top left box.

What is the message?

1.8	172.8	0.714	1300	0.057	2.16
O	E	E	N	T	
0.7×0.9	$4.32 \div 0.08$	0.8^3	46×0.6	$0.08 \div 0.001$	0.08^2
3.6	**80**	**16.86**	**2080**	**54**	**56**
E	O	U	E	F	T
$6^3 \times 0.01$	$0.9^3 - 0.8^2$	0.28×200	$0.4^2 - 0.103$	$0.73 - \dfrac{2}{5}$	4.8×36
27.6	**0.63**	**0.33**	**0.0064**	**0.089**	**0.512**
O	G	H	M	W	R
$19 - 2.14$	$0.144 \div 0.04$	1.7×0.42	$13 \div 0.01$	$0.468 \div 0.26$	5.2×400

2.2 Estimating and checking answers

1 Work out 8×700

2 Work out a rough estimate for 7.93×706

3 Work out 50×9

4 Work out a rough estimate for 51×8.98

5 Answer true or false (the sign $\approx$ means 'is roughly equal to').

(a) 41.2×5.9 (b) $2137 \div 98$ (c) 62×3989

    $\approx 40 \times 6$ $\approx 2000 \div 100$ $\approx 60 \times 4000$

    ≈ 240 ≈ 20 ≈ 24000

6 Do not use a calculator. Decide, by estimating, which of the three answers is closest to the exact answer.

	Calculation	A	B	C
(a)	7.3×31	2100	210	100
(b)	14.9×9.98	150	25	1500
(c)	24.8×40.2	100	1000	200
(d)	19.6×4.94	500	100	10
(e)	6.01×29.8	180	18	360
(f)	59.7×71.1	420	840	4200
(g)	$403 \div 79.12$	32000	50	5
(h)	$899 \div 1.98$	450	1800	45
(i)	$51 \div 0.99$	50	5	200
(j)	$607 \div 21.8$	3	120	30
(k)	$79.3 + 81 + 139$	300	200	400
(l)	9.6×90.4	450	900	90
(m)	$231 + 19.6 + 41.3$	200	390	290
(n)	19.7×31.06	60	300	600
(o)	$\frac{1}{4}$ of (19.86×30.04)	300	150	15
(p)	4.92% of $(7103 - 89)$	350	140	700
(q)	$\frac{11}{21}$ of 10% of 4032	200	400	50
(r)	$\frac{3}{4}$ of 19% of 14.3^2	15	45	30

|

Do not use a calculator for these questions.

1 Gareth needs to buy 19 packets of cereal at £2.49 for each packet. Estimate the total cost.

2 A book weighs 292 g. Estimate how much 31 books would weigh?

3 A book costs £9.95. Estimate the cost of 152 books.

4 Write down each calculation below and match the correct answer from the list given.

(a) $20.6 \div 5$ (b) 49×20.2 (c) 8.1×32

(d) 42×6.8 (e) $2.8 + 13.9$ (f) $3012 \div 4.8$

Answers:	259.2	16.7	898.8	627.5	4.12	285.6

5 Larry works for exactly 40 years. He works for 5 days each week and 8 hours each day. On average he earns 25p for every minute he works. At the end of the 40 years he has saved 10% of the total money he has earned. Estimate how much money he has saved.

6 Caitlin covers 0.79m every time she takes a stride. Estimate the distance she travels if she takes 994 strides.

7 Ryan sells cups of tea for 82p each from his stall. One weekend he sells 396 cups of tea. It costs him £130 to make the tea and sort out the cups. Estimate the profit he makes on selling cups of tea during this weekend.

8

| box of paper £4.95 |
| ink cartridge £13.10 |
| pack of photo paper £7.99 |

Louisa buys 3 boxes of paper, 2 ink cartridges and one pack of photo paper. Roughly how much change would Louisa get from £50?

9 Give an estimate for each of the following calculations

(a) $\dfrac{2109 - 302}{87.4}$ (b) $\dfrac{3}{7}$ of 1362 kg   (c) $\dfrac{19.6^2 - 197}{0.49}$

(d) $\dfrac{4.81 \times 19.7}{13.8 + 11.4}$ (e) 63% of £17983   (f) $\dfrac{9.83 \times 50.03}{0.18}$

|

1 If $56.58 \div 12.3 = 4.6$, would you expect 4.6×12.3 to equal 56.58?
Explain why you chose your answer.

2 Work out the following without using a calculator and check each answer using inverse operations.

(a) $93 - 7.68 = \boxed{}$ check $\boxed{} + 7.68$

(b) $2.94 \times 0.7 = \boxed{}$ check $\boxed{} \div 0.7$

(c) $2.536 \div 0.8 = \boxed{}$ check $\boxed{} \times 0.8$

(d) $1.4 \times 5.6 = \boxed{}$ check $\boxed{} \div 5.6$

(e) $0.8 - 0.034 = \boxed{}$ check $\boxed{} + 0.034$

3   Tom's heart beats around 100000 times each day. Do you think this is likely or unlikely? *Explain* why you chose your answer.

4   Copy and complete with either > or < in the boxes.

(a) $362 \times 0.93 \ \boxed{}\ 362$ (b) $41.8 \times 1.04 \ \boxed{}\ 41.8$ (c) $38 \div 1.3 \ \boxed{}\ 38$

(d) $0.65 \times 0.8 \ \boxed{}\ 0.65$ (e) $102 \div 0.95 \ \boxed{}\ 102$ (f) $1.7 \div 1.4 \ \boxed{}\ 1.7$

5 $\boxed{171.08 \div 47 = 3.64}$

Use the calculation above to work out:

(a) $1710.8 \div 47$ (b) $0.17108 \div 47$ (c) 3.64×47

(d) 36.4×47 (e) $171.08 \div 4.7$ (f) 364×4.7

6 $\boxed{180.04 \div 28 = 6.43}$

Use the calculation above to work out:

(a) $180.04 \div 2.8$ (b) $180.04 \div 0.28$ (c) 6.43×2.8

(d) 64.3×28 (e) 0.643×2.8 (f) $1.8004 \div 0.28$

HWK 2E   **Main Book Page 76**

1   Round off these numbers to one decimal place.

(a) 8.69   (b) 6.46   (c) 7.132   (d) 4.073

(e) 5.243   (f) 10.817   (g) 0.094   (h) 3.044

2   Which of the numbers below round off to 6.78 correct to two decimal places?

$\boxed{6.714}$ $\boxed{6.769}$ $\boxed{6.773}$ $\boxed{6.782}$ $\boxed{6.774}$ $\boxed{6.786}$

3   Work out these answers on a calculator and then round off the answers correct to two decimal places.

(a) $\dfrac{6.99}{2.01}$ (b) $\dfrac{3.8^2}{4.3}$ (c) $\dfrac{8.21}{\sqrt{53}}$ (d) $\dfrac{5.14 \times 3.6}{0.93}$

(e) $\dfrac{5.2}{1.9} + 8.714$ (f) $\dfrac{5.25}{(1.18 + 3.27)}$ (g) $\dfrac{5.06^2}{4.27}$ (h) $\dfrac{3.134}{2.6^2}$

4 Which number below is the smallest which will round off to 8.14 correct to two decimal places?

8.138   8.135   8.141   8.1354   8.1357   8.132

5 How many numbers below round off to 4.8 correct to one decimal place?

4.861   4.841   4.793   4.852   4.768   4.739

6 Give these answers to two decimal places.

(a) $\dfrac{5.16 + 9.3}{3.7}$ (b) $\dfrac{\sqrt{46}}{9} + 3.89$ (c) $\dfrac{7.63}{8.2^2} + \dfrac{5.17}{1.3^2}$ (d) $\dfrac{5.68^2 - 17.4}{\sqrt{32.9}}$

7 What is the smallest number which rounds off to 9.3 correct to one decimal place?

8 What is the smallest number which rounds off to 2.38 correct to two decimal places?

2.3 Geometrical reasoning

| **HWK 1M** | **Main Book Page 79** |

Find the angles marked with letters.

1
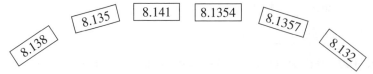
a 126° 86° 79°

2
b 137° 85° 110°

3
e 117° c d 84°

4
f 128° f 78°

5

88° j j 44°

6

58° 101° 92° k

7
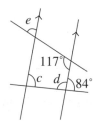
80° l

8

66° q 43° p

9
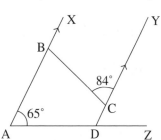
X   Y   Find the values of

B   (a) A$\hat{B}$C   (b) B$\hat{C}$D   (c) A$\hat{D}$C   (d) C$\hat{D}$Z

84°
65° C
A   D   Z

Find the angles marked with letters. Draw each diagram and show your working.

10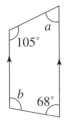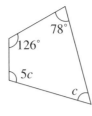

11 a / 105° / b / 68°

12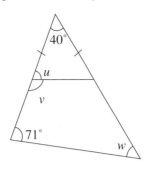

13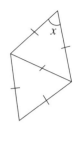

14 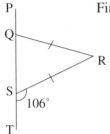 Find the value of QR̂S.

15 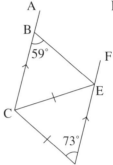 Find the value of BÊC.

HWK 1E ——————————————————————— **Main Book Page 81**

1 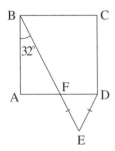 ABCD is a square.
Find the value of DÊF.
Show your working.

2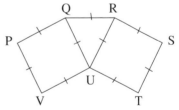

PQUV and RSTU are squares.
Find the value of TÛV. Show your
working.

3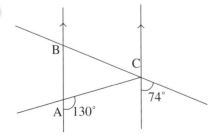

Find the value of AB̂C.
Show your working.

4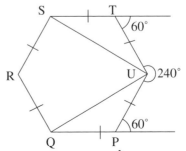

Find the value of SÛQ.

5

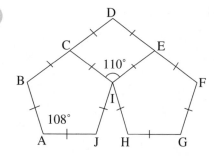

CDEI is a square. (ignore the shape in the diagram) Each angle inside a regular pentagon is 108°. A regular pentagon has equal sides and angles.

Find the value of HÎJ.

6

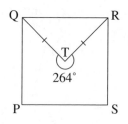

PQRS is a square. Find the value of TR̂S.

7

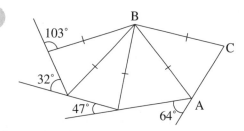

Find the value of AB̂C.

HWK 2M ──────────────────────────── **Main Book Page 82**

Begin each question by drawing a diagram.

1 Calculate the value of angle *n*.

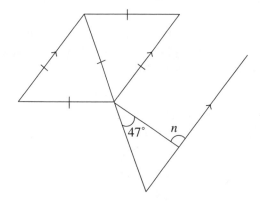

2 BDEA is a square. BĈA is four times as large as larger than BÂC. Calculate the value of CÊD.

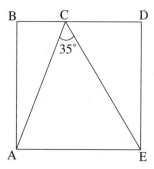

or   BĈA = 4 × BÂC

3 UVST is a square.
Calculate the value of RŜV.

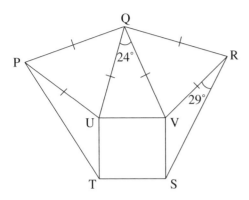

4 BD bisects AB̂C.
Calculate the value of AD̂B.

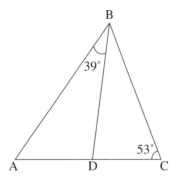

5 Draw a sketch of an isosceles triangle
PQR with PQ = PR. Point Y lies on QR
so that PŶQ = 85°. If PQ̂R = 75°,
calculate the size of RP̂Y.

6 Calculate the value of EĜF.

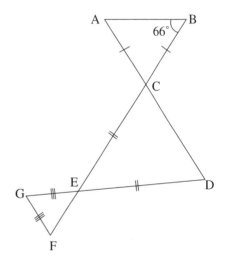

7 PQRT is a parallelogram. SU bisects PŜT. Calculate the value of SÛT.

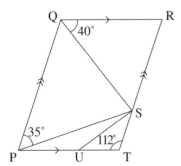

34

1 Copy and complete this proof to show that AD̂C is equal to AB̂C in this kite.

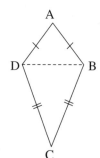

AD̂B = ☐ (angles in isosceles triangle ADB)

BD̂C = ☐ (angles in isosceles triangle BDC)

AD̂C = AD̂B + BD̂C

= ☐ + ☐

= AB̂C

2

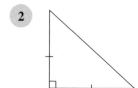

Prove that the angles in a right-angled isosceles triangle are 90°, 45° and 45°.

3 Copy and complete this proof for the sum of the angles in a pentagon.

Draw any pentagon (5 sides) as shown.

a + ☐ + c = 180° (angles in a Δ)

d + e + f = ☐ (angles in a Δ)

g + ☐ + ☐ = ☐ (angles in a Δ)

We must have

a + ☐ + c + d + e + f + g + ☐ + ☐ = ☐

This shows that the sum of the angles in a pentagon is ☐.

4

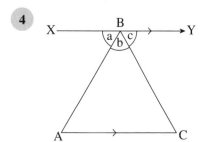

a + b + c = 180° (angles on a straight line)

Prove that the sum of the angles in a triangle is 180°.

2.4 Using algebra

HWK 1M   **Main Book Page 86**

1   Find two matching pairs of expressions

A $\boxed{1 + 2m + 3}$ B $\boxed{2 + m + 4m - 1}$ C $\boxed{2 + 6m - 3m - 1}$

      D $\boxed{7m + 1 - 2m}$ E $\boxed{5m + 4 - 3m}$

2   Simplify the following.

(a) $3m + 7 - 8m$ (b) $3y + 2x - y - 1$ (c) $6m + 3 - 5m - 2n + n$

3   Find an expression for the total distance from A to C.

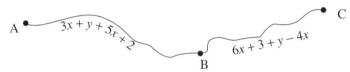

4   Multiply out the brackets.

(a) $4(m + 3)$ (b) $9(2p - 1)$ (c) $3(w + 3q)$ (d) $5(a - 3b)$

5   Copy and complete the following.

(a) $4(\boxed{} + 1) = 8a + 4$ (b) $\boxed{}(2m - 3n) = 12m - \boxed{}$

6   Multiply out the brackets and simplify.

(a) $3(m + 2) + 5(m - 1)$ (b) $4(2n + 3) + 5(n - 2)$

(c) $5(3x + 4) + 2(4x + 3)$ (d) $7(m - 2) + 4(m + 6)$

(e) $4(m + n + 3) + 3(m - n + 2)$ (f) $6(a + 3b - 2c) + 4(2a - b + 4c)$

(g) $5(3x - 2y + 2) + 2(2x + y - 3)$ (h) $4(m - 3 + 2n) + 5(2 + m - n)$

HWK 1E   **Main Book Page 87**

1   In number walls each brick is made by adding the two bricks underneath it.

Draw the walls below and fill in the missing expressions.

(a) 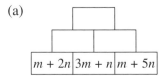   (b) 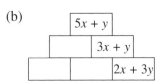   (c)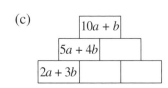

2 Answer true or false.

(a) $4 + m = 4m$

(b) $5p - p = 5$

(c) $m - n = n - m$

(d) $\dfrac{m + m + m}{m} = 3$

(e) $a + b = ab$

(f) $a \times a \times a = a^3$

g) $m^2 + m^2 = m^4$

(h) $3a \times ba = 3a^2b$

(i) $a \times a \div b = \dfrac{2a}{b}$

3 Here are some cards.

$\boxed{a + 3}$ $\boxed{5a}$ $\boxed{a^2}$

$\boxed{a - 1}$ $\boxed{a \div 2}$ $\boxed{a \times a}$ $\boxed{4a - a}$

$\boxed{2a + a + a}$ $\boxed{5 \div a}$ $\boxed{4a}$

(a) Which card is the same as $\boxed{a + a + a}$?

(b) Which card is the same as $\boxed{\dfrac{5}{a}}$?

(c) The card $\boxed{a \times a}$ is the same as the card $\boxed{a^2}$.

Which other pair of cards are the same as each other?

(d) Which card is the same as $\boxed{\dfrac{1}{2}a}$?

(e) What is the difference in the value of the cards $\boxed{a + 3}$ and $\boxed{a - 1}$?

4 Draw these walls like those in question **1** and fill in the missing expressions.

(a)

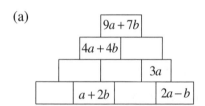

(b)

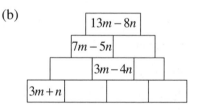

HWK 2E ———————————————————————————— **Main Book Page 90**

1 Here is a flow diagram for the expression $4(2n - 3)$ $\xrightarrow{n} \boxed{\times 2} \xrightarrow{2n} \boxed{-3} \xrightarrow{2n-3} \boxed{\times 4} \xrightarrow{4(2n-3)}$

Find the expression for each of the following flow charts:

(a) $\xrightarrow{n} \boxed{\times 3} \to \boxed{+6} \to \boxed{\times 4} \to$

(b) $\xrightarrow{n} \boxed{\times 5} \to \boxed{-3} \to \boxed{\times 8} \to$

(c) $\xrightarrow{n} \boxed{+4} \to \boxed{\times 3} \to \boxed{+1} \to$

(d) $\xrightarrow{n} \boxed{-2} \to \boxed{\times 9} \to \boxed{-4} \to$

(e) $\xrightarrow{n} \boxed{+5} \to \boxed{\text{square}} \to \boxed{\times 5} \to$

(f) $\xrightarrow{n} \boxed{\text{square}} \to \boxed{+2} \to \boxed{\times 7} \to$

2 Draw the flow diagram for the following expressions.

(a) $6(4n + 1)$ (b) $4(5n - 8)$ (c) $5(n^2 + 4)$

(d) $\dfrac{3n - 6}{7}$ (e) $7(n - 4)^2$ (f) $8(n + 5)^2$

Simplify the expressions in the questions below.

3 $\dfrac{6m}{m}$ **4** $3m^2 - m^2$ **5** $n - 6 + 4n$ **6** $3ab + ba$

7 $\dfrac{n}{3} + \dfrac{n}{3} + \dfrac{n}{3}$ **8** $\dfrac{8x}{2}$ **9** $\dfrac{a \times a}{a}$ **10** $5p - 2 - p - 3$

11 $\dfrac{m^3}{m^4}$ **12** $\dfrac{n + n + n + n}{n}$ **13** $\dfrac{m \times m^2}{m}$ **14** $\dfrac{3a - a}{a}$

15 $\dfrac{m + m + m}{3}$ **16** $\dfrac{a^2 \times 5}{a}$ **17** $\dfrac{n}{5} + \dfrac{n}{5}$

HWK 3M/3E   **Main Book Page 91**

1 Will is paid £7 per hour. How much does he earn if he works for y hours?

2 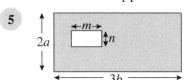 Ryan has two boxes of sweets as shown.

box A   box B

Ryan takes 5 sweets out of box A and 4 sweets out of box B.

(a) How many sweets are left in box A?

(b) How many sweets are left in box B?

(c) What is the total number of sweets left in both boxes?

(d) Ryan now puts one sweet back into box B. How many sweets are now in box B?

3 Mark has £n. Marcus has three times as much money as Mark. Marcus spends £15. How much money does Marcus now have?

4 A bag of crisps costs m pence and a bottle of water costs n pence. Ryan buys x bags of crisps and y bottles of water. How much change will he get if he hands over q pence?

5 Write down an expression for the shaded area.

$2a$ $\leftarrow m \rightarrow$ $\updownarrow n$ $3b$

6 Felix has £$(9n + 23)$. He spends £$(3n + 9)$. He gives half of the remaining money to his sister. How much money does he have left?

7 Jed is selling plates at £m each. He reduces the price of each plate by £2 and sells 29 plates. How much money does he receive?

8 'Sunshine' cereal costs y pence per box. Fresco own brand of the same cereal costs x pence less per box.

How much will 3 'Sunshine' boxes and 5 Fresco boxes cost in total? Simplify your answer.

9

(a) Write down an expression for x in terms of a.

(b) Write down an expression for y in terms of b.

10 Here is a magic square in which the numbers in each row, column and diagonal add up to the same number, in this case 18.

9	4	5
2	6	10
7	8	3

Copy and complete this magic square by first finding the value of n.

	7	$n+7$	
	12	n	5
	1	15	
13	10	4	

2.5 Applying mathematics in a range of contexts 1

HWK 1M/2M/3M/4M/5E/6E ———————————— **Main Book Page 96**

1 Use $\boxed{7}$, $\boxed{4}$, $\boxed{38}$, $\boxed{3}$, $\boxed{-}$, $\boxed{+}$ and $\boxed{\times}$ to make

a calculation which gives the answer 55.

2 A machine makes the same amount of washing powder every minute. It is allowed to run for 9 minutes, after which 2 kg of powder is removed for testing. The remainder is placed in an empty bag labelled A.

The machine is then allowed to run for 5 minutes and all the powder produced in that 5 minutes is put into bag B, which already contains 16 kg.

If bags A and B now contain equal quantities of powder, find the weight of powder produced by the machine every minute.

3

This is a plan of the bottom floor of Bev's house.

She wants to build an extension which will increase the floor area by 15%.

The extension will be square in shape. How long will one side of the square extension need to be?

4 Puja leaves Bristol at 09:25 by train and arrives at London at 11:05. It then takes her 15 minutes to get on a tube train which takes her 23 minutes to get to Earls Court.

Rowan also travels from Bristol to London by train but his journey takes 28% more time than Puja's train journey. It only takes him 11 minutes to catch the tube train which then gets him to Earls Court 3 minutes quicker than Puja's tube journey took.

If Rowan leaves Bristol at 08:13, when does he arrive at Earls Court?

5 The two way table shows how many boys and girls there are in years 7 and 8 in Howton Community School.
What percentage of Year 8 are boys?

(Give your answer to one decimal place)

	boys	girls	total
year 7	118		245
year 8		104	
total			472

6 Work out one quarter of 9% of three tenths of the square root of ten thousand.

7 Some year 8 students were asked how many evenings during the week did they watch three hours or more of TV. The results are shown in the table below.

number of evenings	0	1	2	3	4	5	6	7
frequency	3	3	4	8	11	12	7	5

What percentage of the students watched three hours or more of TV on less than three evenings? (Give your answer to one decimal place)

8

	The Curly Leaf	Fresco
potatoes	£1.85 for 5 lb	78p for 1 kg
apples	£1.62 for 2 lb	£1.58 for 1 kg
carrots	81p for 1.5 lb	£2.40 for 2 kg

1 kg = 2.2 lb (2.2 pounds)

Mark needs to buy 3 kg of potatoes, 1.5 kg of apples and 1.5 kg of carrots.

Which store is it cheaper for Mark to shop in, 'The Curly Leaf' or 'Fresco', and by how much is it cheaper?

40

2.6 Circles

HWK 1M —————————————————————————————————— **Main Book Page 107**

> Remember: circumference = π × diameter

Give all answers to one decimal place.

1. Calculate the circumference of each circle.

(a)

(b)

(c)

(d)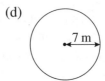

2. A circular pond has a diameter 30 m. Calculate its circumference.

3. A coin has a radius 8 mm. Find its circumference.

4.

   60 m

   Tom walks once around the edge of a 60 m length square field.

   Anna walks once around the edge of an 80 m diameter circular field.

   Who walks further and by how much?

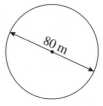

5. In a game show, a comedian lies on a circular turntable. The comedian is 1.7 m tall.

   If the turntable is spun around four complete rotations, how far does the top of the comedian's head travel?

HWK 1E —————————————————————————————————— **Main Book Page 108**

1. The wheels on a bike have a diameter of 59 cm. Alf travels 25 m on this bike. How many times do the wheels go round *completely*?

2.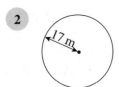

   A dog runs around this circular pond at a speed of 2.5 m/s. How long does it take the dog to run all the way round the pond twice? Give your answer to 1 decimal place.

3. The circumference of a circular field is 400 m. Calculate the diameter of the field to the nearest cm.

4. A circle has a perimeter of 563 cm. Calculate the radius of the circle to the nearest cm.

5 The wheels on Mary's model car have a diameter of 3.2 cm. The wheels on Wayne's model car have a radius of 1.3 cm. Both cars are pushed so that their wheels rotate completely 50 times. How much further does Mary's car travel than Wayne's?

6

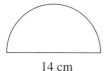

8 cm

$\frac{1}{2}$ cm overlap

12cm

A rectangular piece of paper is wrapped around a tin with a $\frac{1}{2}$ cm overlap for fixing. Calculate the area of the piece of paper. Give your answer to one decimal place.

7 John and his dad go for a bike ride. John's bike wheels have a radius of 49 cm and his dad's bike wheels have a radius of 62 cm. During part of the journey, his dad's bike wheels rotate 530 times. How many complete rotations do John's bike wheels make during the same part of the journey?

HWK 2M ——————————————————————— **Main Book Page 110**

Calculate the perimeter of each shape. All shapes are either semi-circles or quarter circles. Give answers correct to 1 decimal place.

1

14 cm

2

5 cm

3

6.3 cm

4

A   18 cm

Which shape has the longer perimeter and by how much?

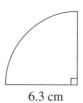

12 cm   B

12 cm

5

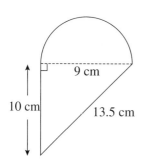

9 cm

10 cm

13.5 cm

This shape is made from a triangle and a semi-circle. Calculate the total perimeter of this shape.

6

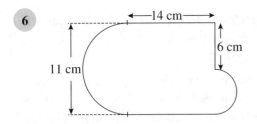

Calculate the perimeter of this shape correct to 1 decimal place.

—14 cm—

6 cm

11 cm

HWK 3M ———————————————————————— **Main Book Page 111**

1 Find the area of a circular road sign with diameter 42 cm.

2 Find the area of a circular plate which has a radius of 11 cm.

3

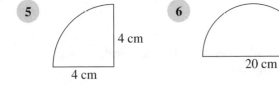

25 cm

A

18 cm

Which shape has the larger area and by how much?

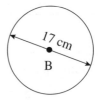

17 cm

B

4

12 cm

12 cm   12 cm

Calculate the shaded area.

In questions **5** to **7** find the area of each shape. All arcs are either semicircles or quarter circles. Give your answers correct to one decimal place.

5

4 cm

4 cm

6

20 cm

7

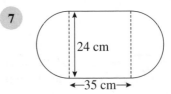

24 cm

←—35 cm—→

8 A circular lawn has diameter 60 m. In the centre of the lawn is a circular pond with a radius of 5 m. What is the area of the lawn without the pond?

Give all answers to one decimal place in this exercise.

1 This shape is made from a rectangle and a quarter circle. Calculate the total area of the shape.

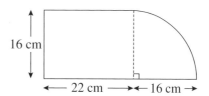

2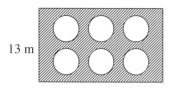

The shaded part of this design is to be painted blue. Each circle has a diameter of 5 m. Calculate the blue area.

3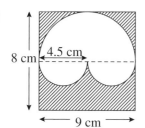

Find the shaded area.

4 shaded area A

Which shaded area is greater and by how much?

shaded area B

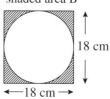

5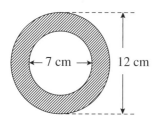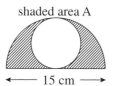

Calculate the shaded area.

UNIT 3

3.1 Reflection

Copy each shape on squared paper and draw the image after reflection in the broken line.

1 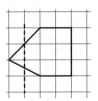　　**2** 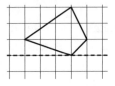　　**3**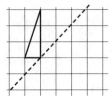

4 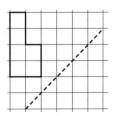　　**5** 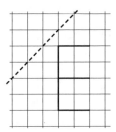　　**6**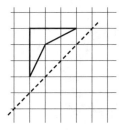

In questions **7** to **9**, copy each shape and draw the image after reflection in the broken line.

7 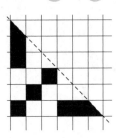　　**8** 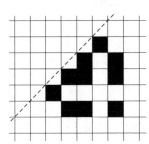　　**9**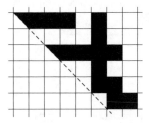

10　First reflect the shape in line 1 and then reflect the image in line 2.

(a) 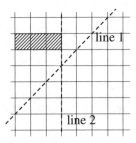　　　　(b)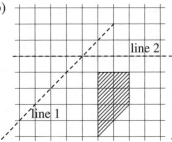

1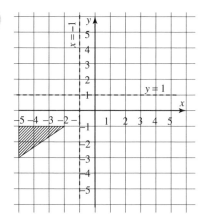

Copy the diagram onto squared paper.

(a) Reflect the shaded triangle in $y = 1$. Label the image P.

(b) Reflect the image P in $x = -1$. Label the new image Q.

(c) Reflect the image Q in $y = 1$. Label the new image R.

2 (a) Draw x and y axes with values from –5 to 5 and draw shape A which has vertices (corners) at (2, 2), (2, 3), (5, 3) and (5, 2).

(b) Reflect shape A in the x-axis. Label the image B.

(c) Reflect shape B in $x = 1$. Label the image C.

(d) Reflect shape C in $y = 1$. Label the image D.

(e) Write down the coordinates of the vertices of shape D.

3 Copy the diagram onto squared paper.

(a) Reflect triangle P in $y = x$. Label the image Q.

(b) Reflect triangle Q in $x = 2$. Label the image R.

(c) Reflect triangle R in the x-axis. Label the image S.

(d) Write down the coordinates of the vertices of triangle S.

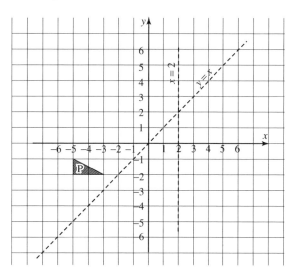

1 (a) Draw x and y axes with values from –5 to 5 and draw triangle A which has vertices at (2, –1), (2, –4) and (3, –4).

(b) Reflect triangle A in the y-axis. Label the image B.

(c) Reflect triangle B in $y = -1$. Label the image C. (Go to next page)

(d) Reflect triangle C in $x = 1$. Label the image D.

(e) Reflect triangle D in $y = x$. Label the image E.

(f) Write down the coordinates of the vertices of triangle E.

2

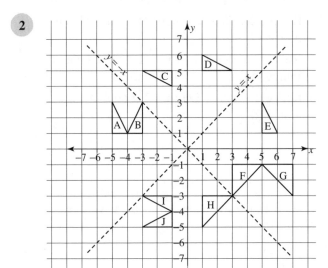

Write down the equation of the mirror line for each of the following reflections

(a) A → B

(b) B → E

(c) I → J

(d) D → E

(e) A → C

(f) C → J

(g) H → F

(h) F → G

3 (a) Find the image of the point (2, 5) after reflection in the line:

(i) $x = 3$ (ii) $x = 40$ (iii) $y = 1$ (iv) $y = 100$ (v) $y = x$

(b) Find the image of the point (m, n) after reflection in the x-axis followed by a reflection in the y-axis.

(c) Find the image of the point (m, n) after reflection in the line $y = -x$.

3.2 Describing data

HWK 1M ──────────────────────────────── **Main Book Page 132**

1 | 5 | 6 | 13 | 8 | 6 | 5 | 8 | 4 | 10 | 4 | 8 |

For the list of numbers above, find

(a) the mean   (b) the median   (c) the mode   (d) the range

2 The numbers below show the scores of ten golfers.

−3, −1, −5, +2, +3, −6, −4, −3, +2, −4

Write down the median score.

3 Which set of numbers below has the greater range?

A 5, −2, 9, 3, −1, 8   or   B −6, 2 ,−2, 5, −3, 6, −4

4 Nine people have weights 52 kg, 63 kg, 51 kg, 48 kg, 62 kg, 59 kg, 60 kg, 62 kg, and 56 kg.

(a) Find the mean weight of the nine people.

(b) Two more people join the group. They weigh 79 kg each. Find the mean weight of all eleven people.

5 Eight people each have one money note as shown below.

| 20 | 10 | 10 | 20 |

| 5 | 20 | 5 | 10 |

Find the mean average amount of money each person has.

HWK 1E ——————————————————————————— **Main Book Page 133**

1 | 3 | 7 | ? | 10 |

The numbers on these cards have a mean average equal to 6. Write down the missing number.

2 The numbers 7, 4, 9, 2, 7 and n have a median equal to 6. Write down the value of n.

3 Nine children get the following marks in a test: 36, 50, 54, 59, 37, 62, 52, 51, 49

Gemma scored the mean average mark. Was she in the bottom half or the top half of this list of marks?

4 Set A: | 8 | 10 | 5 | 9 | 6 | 7 | 4 |

Set B: | 12 | 1 | ? | 8 | 9 |

The mean average of set B is the same as the mean average of set A. Find the missing number.

5 The six numbers below are all positive and have a range of 39. Find the value of n.

15   21   3 n 32   9

6 Seven numbers have a mean of 9 and a median of 8.

| 6 | 6 | 15 | 15 | | | |

Write down three possible missing numbers.

7 The mean of seven numbers is 8. Another number is added to the list making the mean of the eight numbers equal 9. What was the new number that was added to the list?

48

8 The mean weight of 4 girls is 49 kg. The mean weight of 6 boys is 55 kg. Find the mean weight of the 10 boys and girls combined.

9 The mean height of n girls is p metres. The mean height of m boys is q metres. Write down an expression for the mean height of all the boys and girls combined.

10 Here are 6 cards and you are told that x is a positive whole number.

| $x + 3$ | $x - 3$ | $3x + 3$ |
| $4x + 7$ | $x + 5$ | $x + 2$ |

(a) Find, in terms of x,

    (i)   the median of the 6 cards

    (ii)   the range of the 6 cards

    (iii) the mean of the 6 cards

(b) The range is 8 greater than the median. Find the value of x.

HWK 2M ——————————————————————— **Main Book Page 135**

1 Children in class 8A are given a maths test. Their marks are recorded below.

17   23   19   28   15   17   22   28   19   20
24   8   21   15   28   16   27   29   21   23

(a) Find the mean mark and the range of the marks.

(b) Children in class 8B took the same test. Their mean mark was 24 and the range of the marks was 12. Use the means and the ranges to compare the test marks for classes 8A and 8B.

2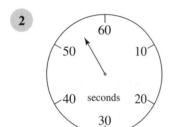

Two groups of people were asked to estimate when one minute had passed. Their estimates are shown in the boxes below. The times are given in seconds.

| Group X | 54 | 61 | 60 | 55 | 62 | 66 | 61 | 51 | 52 |

| Group Y | 59 | 58 | 67 | 50 | 63 | 69 | 71 | 67 |

(a) Work out the mean estimate and the range for group X.

(b) Work out the mean estimate and the range for group Y.

(c) Write one or two sentences to compare the estimates for the two groups.

3 Two groups of young children were asked how much pocket money they received each week. The results are shown below:

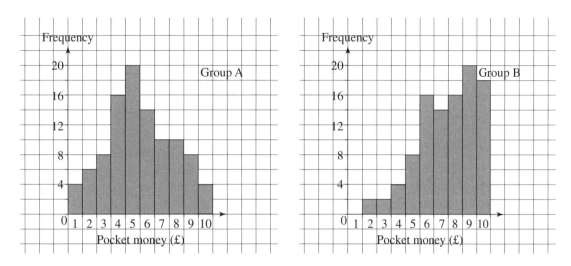

Write down one or two sentences to compare the weekly pocket money received by children in Group A and Group B.

HWK 2E ———————————————————————— **Main Book Page 137**

1 The frequency table shows the weights of 50 apples in a box.

weight	90 g	100 g	110 g	120 g	130 g
frequency	8	11	17	9	5

(a) Calculate the mean weight of the apples.

(b) Find the modal weight of the apples (ie. the mode)

(c) Find the median weight of the apples.

2 40 children were asked how many drinks of water they had during one day. The findings are shown in the frequency table below.

number of drinks	0	1	2	3	4	5	6
frequency	3	5	6	7	12	5	2

(a) Calculate the mean number of drinks.

(b) Find the modal number of drinks (ie. the mode).

(c) Find the median number of drinks.

3 Tom wants to know if a 'city' family or a 'village' family spends more or less each week on food. He asks 25 families in a city and 25 families in a village. The results are shown in the frequency tables on the next page.

city	
food bill (£)	frequency
80	0
100	4
120	8
140	6
160	7

village	
food bill (£)	frequency
80	5
100	5
120	10
140	4
160	1

(a) Calculate the mean weekly food bill for the 'city' families.

(b) Calculate the mean weekly food bill for the 'village' families.

(c) Which group of families spends more each week on food? Can you suggest a possible reason for this?

4 The table shows the number of cars owned by some families in a street.

(a) If the modal number of cars is 2, find the largest possible value of n.

(b) If the mean number of cars is 2.28, find n.

number of cars	frequency
1	5
2	11
3	n
4	3

HWK 3M ──────────────────────────── **Main Book Page 139**

1 25 people are asked how many DVDs they have. The results are shown below.

15	21	41	43	38
8	23	34	47	16
22	38	43	20	6
33	21	19	8	23
34	12	43	16	37

Draw an ordered stem and leaf diagram. Three entries are shown below.

Stem	Leaf
0	
1	5
2	1
3	
4	1

Remember the key, for example: 1 | 2 means 12

2 The numbers shown below give the ages of 30 people on a train between Birmingham and Derby. Draw an ordered stem and leaf diagram to show this data.

24	48	17	58	52	40	64	57	69	28
67	58	32	66	13	68	59	37	10	66
63	21	19	48	57	69	17	58	67	24

3 The stem and leaf diagrams below show the weights of the players in two rugby teams.

Halford	
Stem	Leaf
8	3 8 9
9	2 5 6 6 8
10	6 7 7
11	3 4 6
12	1

Key
9 | 5 means 95 kg

Malby	
Stem	Leaf
8	0 2
9	4 8 9
10	6 7 7 7
11	2 5 5 8
12	4 9

Key
10 | 7 means 107 kg

(a) Find the range and median weight of the rugby players for each team.

(b) Write two sentences to compare the weights of the rugby players in each team (One sentence should involve how spread out the weights are (range) and the second sentence should involve an average (median)).

4 A group of children are drawing with pencils. The stem and leaf diagram opposite shows the length of each pencil.

(a) What is the median pencil length?

(b) Write down the range.

Stem	Leaf
7	4 6
8	3 5 5
9	0 2 4 4 7
10	2 6 7 7
11	4 5 8 8 8
12	3 4 5 5 9 9
13	2 2 6 7

Key
9 | 4 means 9.4 cm

3.4 Using formulas and expressions

HWK 1M ———————————————————— **Main Book Page 147**

In questions **1** to **10** you are given a formula. Find the value of the letter required in each case.

1 $a = 4b - 3$

Find a when $b = 5$

2 $p = 9w + 7$

Find p when $w = 6$

3 $y = 3x + 12$

Find y when $x = 5$

4 $m = \frac{n}{4} - 8$

Find m when $n = 48$

5 $a = \frac{b}{10} + 4$

Find a when $b = 30$

6 $y = 2(6x + 3)$

Find y when $x = 9$

7 $m = 7(4n - 1)$

Find m when $n = 6$

8 $a = \frac{8b - 4}{10}$

Find a when $b = 8$

9 $y = 3(9x + 2)$

Find y when $x = 2$

10 $p = \frac{w}{7} + 20$

Find p when $w = 28$

11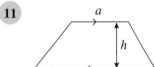

The area A of this trapezium is given by the formula

$A = \frac{1}{2}h(a + b)$

Find the value of A when $h = 10$, $a = 3$ and $b = 9$.

12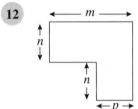

The total area A of this shape is given by the formula

$A = n(m + p)$

Find the value of A when $n = 20$, $m = 40$ and $p = 15$.

13 $w = p^2 + 7p$

Find w when $p = 9$

14 $a = \frac{29 - 4n}{10}$

Find a when $n = 7$

15 $y = 4x(100 - x^2)$

Find y when $x = 5$

16 $m = p^3 + p^2 + p$

Find m when $p = 6$

HWK 1E   **Main Book Page 147**

1   In the formulas below x is given in terms of m and n. Find the value of x in each case.

(a) $x = mn + 8n$ when $m = -9$ and $n = 6$

(b) $x = m^2 - 4n$ when $m = -6$ and $n = -2$

(c) $x = m(3m - 6)$ when $m = -3$

2   Norman sells chocolates. Each month he buys n boxes of chocolates to sell at £9 for each box. He always gives one box to his partner and one box to each of his two children. Norman gets £m for selling the remaining boxes given by the formula

$$m = 9(n - 3)$$

Find the value of m when

(a) $n = 43$ (b) $n = 60$ (c) $n = 100$

3 Find the value of y using the formulas and values given.

(a) $p = xy - 6$ when $x = 7$ and $y = -2$

(b) $y = (3x - 1)^2$ when $x = -4$

(c) $w = mn + n^2 - 8$ when $m = -3$ and $n = -4$

(d) $x = \dfrac{n^2 + 3n}{2n}$ when $n = -9$

4  The surface area A of a sphere is approximately given by the formula

$A = 12r^2$

Find the surface area of a sphere with a radius of $\frac{3}{4}$ cm.

5 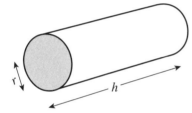 The total surface area A of a cylinder is approximately given by the formula

$A = 6r(h + r)$

Find the total surface area A of a cylinder with $r = \frac{2}{3}$ cm and $h = 1\frac{1}{2}$ cm.

6 If you add the numbers $1 + m + m^2 + m^3 + \ldots + m^n$, the sum is given by the formula:

$$\text{Sum} = \frac{1 - m^{n+1}}{1 - m}$$

(a) Use the formula to work out $1 + 3 + 3^2 + \ldots + 3^{10}$

(b) Check your answer by adding the numbers in the normal way.

(c) Use the formula to work out $1 + 2 + 4 + 8 + \ldots + 8192$

7 This open box has no top.
The surface area A is given by the formula

$A = 2np + mn + 2mp$

Find the value of p if $n = 6$, $m = 7$ and $A = 146$.

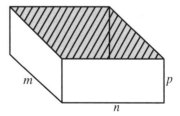

HWK 2M ━━━━━━━━━━━━━━━━━━━━━━━━━ **Main Book Page 151**

1 For each statement answer 'true' or 'false'

(a) $4t - t = 3t$ (b) $m + m = m^2$ (c) $\dfrac{4n + 2n}{n} = 6$

(d) $3(n-3) = 3n - 6$ (e) $m \div 3 = 3 \div m$ (f) $\frac{m}{n} - \frac{w}{n} = \frac{m-w}{n}$

(g) $4n + n = 4n^2$ (h) $6a - a = 6$ (i) $m - n + p = -n + p + m$

2 Which of the cards below have a value of 15 when $x = 4$?

| $3x + 4$ | $x^2 - 1$ | $20 - x$ | $(x-1)^2 + 6$ |

| $\dfrac{30x}{8}$ | $2x + 9$ | $5x - 5$ |

3 Find the value of each expression.

(a) $8 - 2x$ if $x = 3$ (b) $\frac{x}{5} + 4$ if $x = 40$

(c) $3(4 + 2y)$ if $y = 10$ (d) $n^2 - 19$ if $n = 8$

(e) $\frac{4x}{3} - 16$ if $x = 12$ (f) $\frac{n-6}{n}$ if $n = 10$

(g) $\frac{m+6}{m+1}$ if $m = 4$ (h) $x^3 - 17$ if $x = 3$

(i) $(n-4)^3$ if $n = 11$ (j) $\frac{3}{n} - \frac{1}{2}$ if $n = 4$

4 Find the value of $\dfrac{\left(\frac{6}{n} + \frac{9}{n}\right)^2}{n+2}$ if $n = 3$.

HWK 2E   **Main Book Page 152**

1 Given that $w = -5$ and $x = 9$, find the value of each of the following expressions.

(a) $x - w$ (b) $x^2 + w$ (c) $4(w + x)$

(d) xw (e) $2w + x$ (f) $w^2 + 3$

(g) $x(3x + w)$ (h) $\dfrac{10x}{w}$ (i) $w(2x - w)$

2 If $n = -2$, which expression has the larger value?

| $5n - n$ | or | $2(4n + 3)$ |

3 Given that $m = -3$ and $n = -4$, find the value of each of the following expressions.

(a) $4m + n$ (b) $m^2 - n$ (c) $n(2m + 5)$

(d) $mn + m^2$ (e) $n^2 - m^2$ (f) $4m(5n + 3)$

(g) $n^3 + 4m$ (h) $(3m + 8)^2 - 2n$ (i) $m(n + 7) - n(m + 3)$

4 Write down these six expressions in order of size when $n = -3$, starting with the smallest.

| $(3n - 1)^2 + n^2$ | $n^3 + (n - 1)^2$ | $6(2n + 1) - (n - 4)$ |

| $\dfrac{5(3 + 2n)}{3}$ | $(5n + 10)^2 - 6n$ | $n^3 - (2n - 3)^2$ |

3.5 Construction and locus

You need a ruler, protractor and pair of compasses.

1. Construct triangle ABC as shown.
   Use a protractor to measure $A\hat{B}C$.

   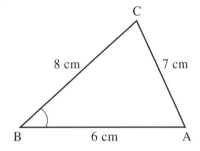

2. Construct each triangle and measure the side x.

   (a)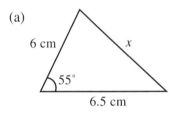

   (b)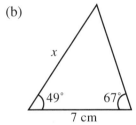

   (c)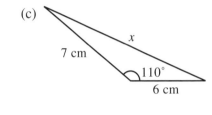

3. Construct rhombus PQRS as shown.
   Use a protractor to measure $P\hat{Q}R$.

   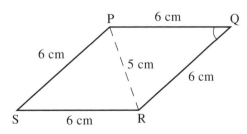

4.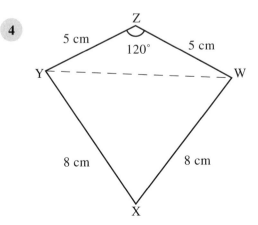

   Construct the kite WXYZ. Use a protractor to measure $W\hat{X}Y$.

> Remember: The *locus* of a point is the path traced out by the point as it moves.

1 Mark a point A with a cross. Hundreds of ants stand exactly 6 cm from the point A. Draw a diagram to show this.

2 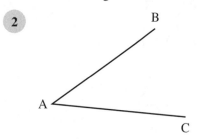 Copy this diagram. The ants now move so that each ant is exactly the same distance from line AB as line AC. Show this on your diagram.

3 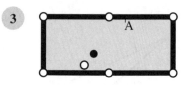 This diagram shows a white ball and black ball on a snooker table. Copy the diagram. Darryl hits the white ball against the black ball. The black ball hits the side of the table at A then goes down the hole in the bottom right-hand corner. Darryl is very surprised. Show what happens to the black ball on your diagram.

4 Draw another copy of the snooker table with the black ball in the same starting position. If the black ball goes down a different hole, show what happens to the black ball on your diagram. *Describe* what happens to the black ball and which hole it goes down.

5 On a clock, the time goes from 10:00 to 10:20. Describe the *locus* of the tip of the minute hand.

6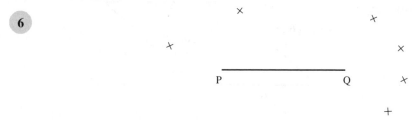

All the crosses shown above are 1.5 cm away from the line PQ. Copy the diagram and draw the locus of *all* the points 1.5 cm away from the line PQ.

7 Shade the locus of all the points which are less than or equal to 3 cm from a fixed point P.

8 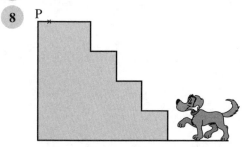 A dog with a bone in its mouth runs up these stairs and drops the bone on the point marked P. Copy the stairs and draw a rough sketch of the locus of the bone as it travels from the bottom of the stairs to the point P.

9 Mark two points P and Q which are 3 cm apart. Draw the locus of points which are an equal distance (equidistant) from P and Q.

● P

● Q

10

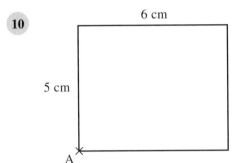

6 cm

5 cm

A

Copy this diagram. Draw the locus of points which are 4 cm from A and are inside the rectangle.

| **HWK 3M** | **Main Book Page 158** |

You need a ruler, protractor and pair of compasses.

1 Draw a horizontal line PQ of length 7 cm. Construct the perpendicular bisector of PQ.

2 Draw a vertical line XY of length 6 cm. Construct the perpendicular bisector of XY.

3 Draw a line and a point Y on the line. Construct the perpendicular from the point Y.

4 • A

Copy this diagram and construct the line which passes through A and is perpendicular to the line.

5

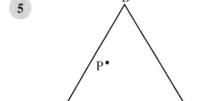

B

P•

A   C

Copy this diagram. Construct 3 lines through P, one line being perpendicular to each of the 3 sides of the triangle.

58

1   Draw an angle of about 50°. Construct the bisector of the angle.

2   (a) Construct the perpendicular bisector of a
line AB as shown. Label the bisector
CD. Label the point Y as shown.

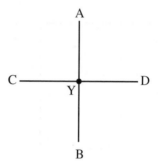

(b) Construct the bisector of AŶD.

(c) Construct the bisector of BŶD.

(d) Label the bisectors as shown opposite.

(e) Use your protractor to measure CŶX.

(f) Use your protractor to measure AŶZ.

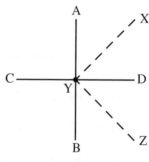

3   Use a ruler and compasses only to construct an angle of $22\frac{1}{2}°$.

4   Using ruler and compasses only construct an angle of 60° (think about the angles in an
equilateral triangle).

5

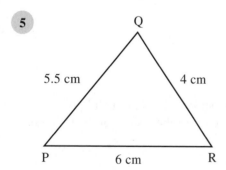

(a) Use a ruler and compasses only to construct triangle
PQR as shown.

(b) Construct the angle bisector of QP̂R. Label this line PX.

(c) Construct the angle bisector of PR̂Q. Label this line RY.

(d) Use your protractor to measure QP̂X and PR̂Y.

UNIT 4

4.1 Bearings and scale drawing

1

North

Q

115° 160°

85°

North

65°

255° 40°

P

North

20°

55°

R 285°

Write down the bearing of:

(a) Q from P

(b) R from Q

(c) R from P

(d) P from R

2 Measure the bearing of   (a) A to B   (b) C to D   (c) E to F   (d) G to H
(e) I to J   (f) K to L   (g) M to N

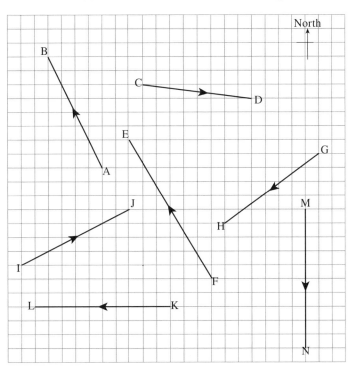

3 Draw lines to show the following bearings.

    (a) 065°   (b) 170°   (c) 250°   (d) 155°   (e) 310°

4 A ship sails from A to P then to B. Another ship sails from C to Q then to D.

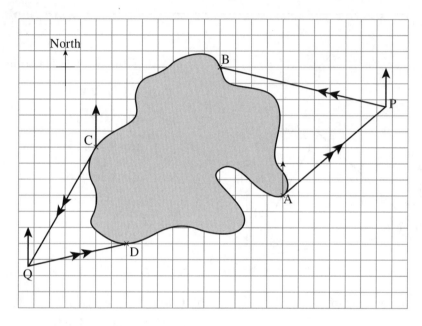

    (a) Measure the bearing of A to P.

    (b) Measure the bearing of P to B.

    (c) Measure the bearing of C to Q.

    (d) Measure the bearing of Q to D.

5 North

    (a) Write down the bearing of B from A.

    (b) Write down the bearing of A from B.

    North

    140°

    A

    40°

    B

6 The bearing of point P from point Q is 105°. What is the bearing of point Q from point P?

7 The bearing of point X from point Y is 230°. What is the bearing of point Y from point X?

HWK 1E   **Main Book Page 175**

In questions ① to ⑤ use a scale of 1 cm to represent 1 km. Draw an accurate scale drawing to help you answer each question.

1   A ship sails 7 km due north and then a further 5 km on a bearing 075°.

How far is the ship now from its starting point?

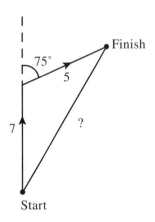

2   A ship sails 6 km due north and then a further 6 km on a bearing 080°.

How far is the ship now from its starting point?

3   Sarah and Barclay are standing at the same point A. Sarah walks for 7 km on a bearing of 050°. Barclay walks for 6 km on a bearing of 310°. How far is Sarah from Barclay now?

4   A ship sails due south for 6 km and then on a bearing of 120° for 3 km. How far is the ship now from its starting point?

5   Draw a point P with a cross.
Point Q is 7 km from P on a bearing of 072° from P.
Point R is 5 km from P on a bearing of 190° from P.
What is the bearing of R from Q?

6   Use a scale of 1 cm for 10 km. Palton is 100 km from Beale on a bearing of 090°.
A group of hikers is on a bearing of 045° from Beale and on a bearing of 325° from Palton.

(a) Make a scale drawing to show the position of the hikers.

(b) The group of hikers now travel 30 km on a bearing of 255°.
What is the bearing of the hikers from Beale now?

7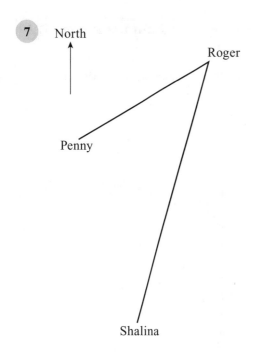

Penny is 20 km from Roger on a bearing of 245°.
Shalina is 35 km from Roger on a bearing of 205°.

(a) Draw an accurate diagram using a scale of 1 cm
for 5 km.

(b) Penny now travels 15 km on a bearing of 200°.
Shalina travels 25 km on a bearing of 065°.
How far now is Penny from Shalina and what
is the bearing of Penny from Shalina?

4.3 Handling data

| HWK 1M/2M/2E | Main Book Page 180 |

1 The scatter graph shows the
waist sizes and weights of some
people.

(a) How many people weighed more
than 70 kg?

(b) How many people had a waist
size of less than 36 inches?

(c) Answer *true* or *false*: 'In general
as waist size increases, weight
increases.'

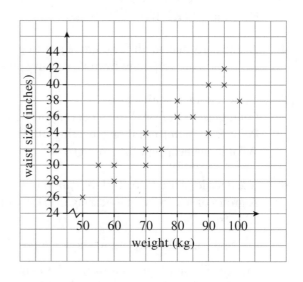

2 The scatter graph shows the heights of
some people and how many shirts they
own.

(a) How many people are more than
150 cm tall?

(b) How many people own less than
8 shirts?

(c) Answer *true* or *false*: 'In general as
the number of shirts increases,
height increases.'

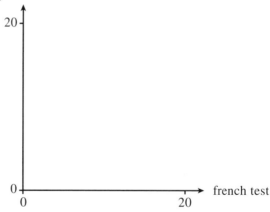

3

french test	german test
13	14
19	17
16	17
8	8
16	15
3	4
10	11
20	19
18	18
7	5
11	12
18	19
10	8
12	10
9	9
15	16

The table shows two test scores obtained by
16 children in Year 8 for french and german

(a) Draw the axes shown below and
complete the scatter graph.

german test

20

0

0   20   french test

(b) Describe the correlation, if any.

4 Describe the correlation, if any, in these scatter graphs.

(a)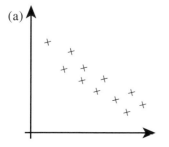

(b)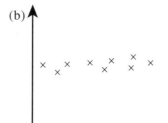

(c)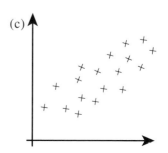

64

5 If scatter graphs were drawn with the quantities below on the two axes, what sort of correlation would you expect to see in each case?

(a) salary; value of home lived in

(b) maths ability; shoe size

(c) number of pages in a book; time to read the book

(d) petrol used by a car; further distance that a car may travel

(e) time spent by a person at the gym; time the person takes to run 5 miles

HWK 3M/3E ──────────────────────────── **Main Book Page 186**

1 The heights of two groups of teenagers are measured. The heights for each group are shown in the frequency diagrams below.

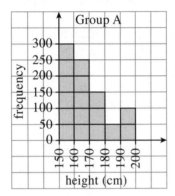
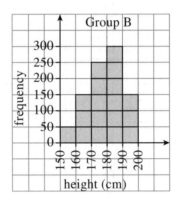

(a) Which group of teenagers is generally taller?

(b) Which frequency diagram would you expect if you measured the heights of all the teenagers in a Sixth Form College? Explain your answer.

2 (a) 18 ten-year-old children run a 400 metre race. Their times (in seconds) are shown below.

64, 63, 86, 75, 81, 92, 74, 77, 85, 93, 76, 65, 84, 91, 73, 83, 76, 75

Put the heights into groups.

class interval	frequency
$60 \leq t < 70$	
$70 \leq t < 80$	
$80 \leq t < 90$	
$90 \leq t < 100$	

(b) Draw a frequency diagram like those in question **1**.

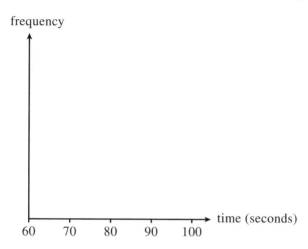

(c) The same children run a 400 metre race when they are seventeen years old.

Their times t (in seconds) are shown below.

67, 56, 65, 57, 53, 74, 59, 53, 71

68, 52, 66, 75, 61, 54, 62, 56, 63

Put the heights into groups similar to part (a).

(d) Draw a frequency diagram like those in question **1**.

(e) Write a sentence to compare the times shown by each frequency diagram. Suggest a reason for the difference.

3 72 people were asked what their favourite type of chocolate was. The results are shown in the table below.

type of chocolate	frequency
milk	32
dark	30
white	10

(a) Work out the angle on a pie chart for one person.

(b) Work out the angle for each type of chocolate and draw a pie chart.

4

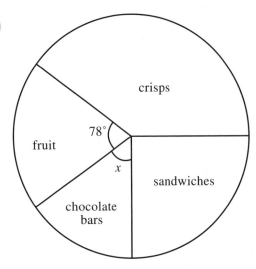

Year 8 children who bring packed lunches to school are asked what main items they have in their lunch. The pie chart opposite shows the results.

40% of items are crisps and $\frac{1}{4}$ are sandwiches.

Calculate the size of angle x in the pie chart.

5 900 pupils in Cork Field School and 350 pupils in Manor High School were asked what they enjoyed doing most at weekends. The results are shown in the two pie charts.

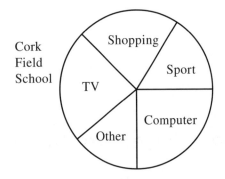

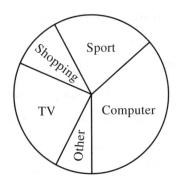

Did more pupils in Manor High School choose using the computer than pupils in Cork Field School or less? *Explain* your answer.

4.4 Fractions, decimals, percentages

| HWK 1M | Main Book Page 193 |

1 Answer true or false.

(a) $0.03 = \frac{3}{100}$ (b) $\frac{3}{5} = 0.35$ (c) $\frac{17}{20} = 0.85$

(d) $0.34 = \frac{3}{4}$ (e) $\frac{70}{100} = 0.7$ (f) $\frac{8}{25} = 0.32$

2 Change the following decimals to fractions, cancelling when possible.

(a) 0.2   (b) 0.09   (c) 0.36   (d) 0.75   (e) 0.007

(f) 0.025   (g) 0.73   (h) 0.008   (i) 0.45   (j) 0.16

3 Change the following mixed numbers to decimals.

(a) $4\frac{2}{5}$ (b) $3\frac{11}{20}$ (c) $7\frac{19}{50}$ (d) $1\frac{13}{25}$ (e) $6\frac{1}{8}$

4 For each pair of numbers, write down which is the larger.

(a) $\frac{7}{10}$ 0.8   (b) 0.94 $\frac{19}{20}$ (c) 0.17 $\frac{3}{20}$

(d) 0.26 $\frac{7}{25}$ (e) $\frac{3}{50}$ 0.04   (f) $\frac{9}{25}$ 0.49

5 Write these numbers in order of size, smallest first.

$\frac{17}{20}$,   0.75, $\frac{9}{10}$, $\frac{18}{25}$,   0.77,   0.735

HWK 3M/3E ———————————————————————— **Main Book Page 197**

1 | $\frac{7}{20}$ $\frac{6}{25}$ $\frac{9}{40}$ $\frac{1}{4}$ |

Change each fraction into a percentage then write these fractions in order of size, starting with the smallest.

2 Change these decimals to percentages.

(a) 0.33   (b) 0.64   (c) 0.09   (d) 0.14   (e) 1.3

3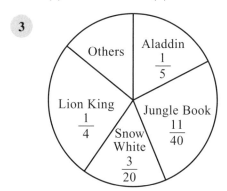

Some people were asked what their favourite Disney cartoon was. The pie chart shows the results.

(a) What percentage prefer Snow White?

(b) What percentage prefer Jungle Book?

(c) What is the difference between the percentages for Jungle Book and the Lion King?

(d) What percentage prefer 'others'?

4 Use a calculator to change these fractions to percentages, rounding to the nearest whole number.

(a) $\frac{4}{17}$ (b) $\frac{5}{9}$ (c) $\frac{6}{7}$ (d) $\frac{5}{11}$ (e) $\frac{19}{22}$

5 Jack eats $\frac{9}{13}$ of his food. What percentage of his food does he leave? (give your answer to the nearest whole number)

6

| 80% | $\frac{12}{150}$ | 26% | $\frac{4}{5}$ | 16% | 0.65 | $\frac{15}{40}$ | 75% | $\frac{3}{25}$ |

0.48								0.08
0.75								$\frac{16}{20}$
$\frac{12}{25}$								$\frac{3}{8}$
$\frac{13}{20}$								65%
0.34								$\frac{21}{28}$
$\frac{13}{50}$								$\frac{2}{25}$
37.5%								$\frac{39}{150}$

Each number belongs to a group of 4 equivalent numbers (two fractions, one decimal and one percentage).

Write down each group of 4 numbers.

Beware: there are 4 numbers which do *not* belong to any group.

| 0.26 | $\frac{36}{75}$ | $\frac{12}{65}$ | 8% | $\frac{3}{4}$ | 0.8 | 48% | $\frac{52}{80}$ | 0.375 |

7 Write in order of size, smallest first.

42%, $\quad \frac{9}{20}$, $\quad \frac{8}{19}$, $\quad$ 0.405, $\quad 44\frac{1}{2}\%$, $\quad \frac{15}{38}$

8 Which is larger and by how much?

$\boxed{39\% \text{ of } 3\frac{2}{3}}$ or $\boxed{0.7 \times 2\frac{1}{20}}$

HWK 4M/4E ———————————————————— **Main Book Page 199**

1 Work out

(a) 5% of £40

(b) $2\frac{1}{2}\%$ of £40

(c) $7\frac{1}{2}\%$ of £40

(d) $17\frac{1}{2}\%$ of £40

(e) $17\frac{1}{2}\%$ of £120

(f) $17\frac{1}{2}\%$ of £60

2 John buys a house for £294 000. He has to pay a 2.5% tax called stamp duty. How much tax does he pay?

3 A United Nations army unit is to be made up from soldiers from four nations as shown in the table.

Country	size of available force	Percentage chosen
UK	1600	3%
Germany	400	7%
Spain	250	12%
New Zealand	1400	2%

(a) Write down how many soldiers are chosen from each country.

(b) From which country did the highest number of soldiers come?

4 Work out, giving each answer correct to the nearest penny.

(a) 26% of £5.19

(b) 31% of £16.46

(c) 8.5% of £29.12

(d) 3.4% of £19.74

5 The cost of a £49 train ticket to London is increased by 4%. What is the new cost of the ticket?

6 (a) Increase £160 by 18%. (b) Decrease £65 by 9%.

7 Joe has £42 and spends 63% of his money. Beth has £73 and spends 78% of her money. Who has more money left and by how much?

8 Terry is building a garage and has used 350 bricks so far. He needs to use a further 82% of the bricks used so far. How many bricks will he use in total?

9

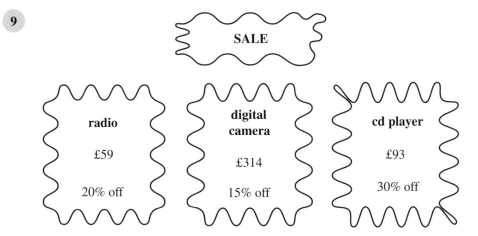

Hannah buys all 3 items above in the sale. How much does she pay in total?

10 Molly's gas bill is £114 plus an extra 5% VAT (known as Value Added Tax). How much does Molly have to pay in total?

70

Reminder: The quick way to work out the new value after a percentage increase/decrease
is as follows:

Decrease £280 by 18%

New value = 82% of £280

$= 0.82 \times 280$

$= £229.60$

0.82 is called the 'multiplier'.

Use this quick method to answer the questions in this exercise.

1. (a) Decrease £340 by 3%   (b) Increase £520 by 7%

   (c) Increase £1290 by 4.5%   (d) Reduce £670 by 12.4%

2. Marvin is trying to sell his car for £2500. He is not having much luck so decides to knock 15% off the selling price. How much is he asking for his car now?

3. Lucy's garage bill is £210 plus an extra 17.5% VAT (known as Value Added Tax). How much does Lucy have to pay in total?

4.

Last year
Cornet £1.80
Sales 1060

This year
Cornet price increased by 20%
Sales decrease by 20%

Each year Alfonso sells ice-creams at the Banwell festival.

   (a) Did Alfonso make more money, the same money or less money on selling cornets this year compared to last year?

   (b) Write down the difference in the amount of money he made.

5. Tania sells cabbages at 90p each and galia melons at £1.60 each. Towards the end of the day she reduces the price of a cabbage by 30% and the price of a melon by 25%.

   She then sells 14 cabbages and 9 melons. How much money does she receive in total for these cabbages and melons?

6. Alex buys a table for £350 and sells it one week later for a 45% profit. The person who buys the table then sells it on at a 20% loss. How much does this person sell the table for?

7

Hal invests £5000 and makes an 8% profit after one year. He leaves all the money invested and makes a further 7% profit one year later.

How much money does he now have in total?

£5000

4.5 Interpreting and sketching real life graphs

| HWK 1M/1E | Main Book Page 203 |

1 A liquid is poured at a constant rate into this container until the container is completely full. Sketch a graph to show how the liquid level rises as the liquid is poured into the container.

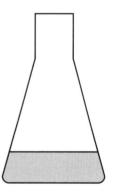

2

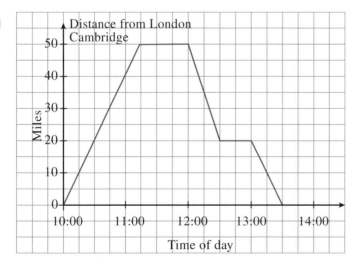

The graph above shows Alan's journey from London to Cambridge.

(a) When did he arrive at Cambridge?

(b) How long did he stop at Cambridge?

P.T.O.

(c) When did he arrive back in London?

(d) Find Alan's speed on his journey from London to Cambridge.

(e) On his way back to London, Alan stops for half an hour. What is his speed for the final 20 miles of his journey?

3

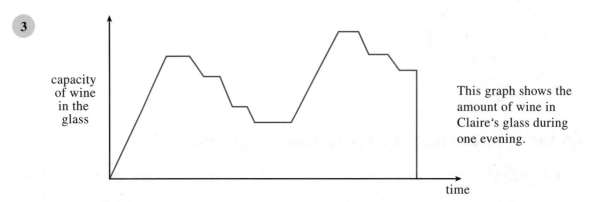

capacity of wine in the glass

This graph shows the amount of wine in Claire's glass during one evening.

time

(a) How many times do you think the glass was filled up with wine?

(b) Explain the shape of the graph. What do the horizontal lines and sloping lines suggest?

(c) What do you think happened at the end?

4 Maggie has a peach tree. In the morning she picks a peach and places it on a window ledge in her kitchen. It is a very hot and sunny day.

In the evening she decides to put the peach in her freezer.

Sketch a graph to show the temperature of the peach during the day.

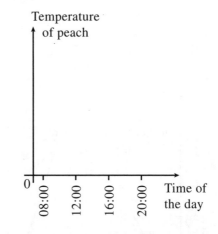

Temperature of peach

0   08:00   12:00   16:00   20:00   Time of the day

5 A person jumps out of an aeroplane and freefalls before opening a parachute. He then glides to the ground. Sketch a graph to show how quickly he heads towards the ground.

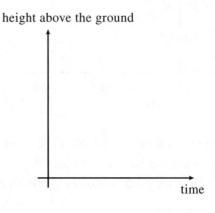

height above the ground

time

6 Draw a vertical axis on squared paper which goes up to 10 km. Draw a horizontal axis which goes up to 5 hours.

Lucy leaves her house and walks for 1 hour at 4 km/h. She then stops at a shop for $\frac{1}{2}$ hour. She then walks at 6 km/h for $\frac{1}{2}$ hour.

She now walks a further 1 km which takes her another $\frac{1}{2}$ hour. At this point she walks directly home at a speed of 4 km/h.

Draw a travel graph to show Lucy's journey. When did she get back to her house?

4.6 Rotation and combined transformations

| HWK 1M/1E | Main Book Page 208 |

In questions **1** to **3** draw the shape and then draw and shade its new position (the image), after the rotation stated. Take O as the centre of rotation in each case.

1

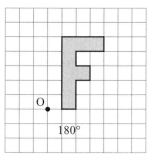

180°

2

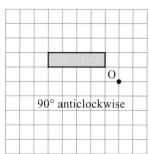

90° anticlockwise

3

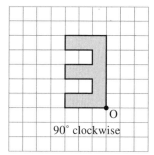

90° clockwise

4 Copy the diagram shown, using axes from −6 to 6.

(a) Rotate shape P 90° anticlockwise about (0, 0). Label the new shape R.

(b) Rotate triangle Q 90° clockwise about (4, −1). Label the new shape S.

(c) Rotate shape Q 180° about (0, 0). Label the new shape T.

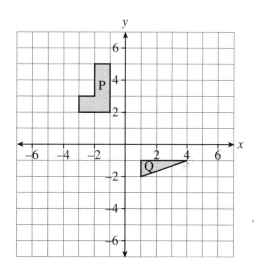

5 (a) Draw axes with values from –6 to 6 and draw triangle P with vertices at (–3, –2), (–3, –6) and (–5, –2).

(b) Rotate triangle P 90° anticlockwise about (0, 0). Draw and label the new triangle Q.

(c) Rotate triangle Q 90° anticlockwise about (2, –2). Draw and label the new triangle R.

(d) Rotate triangle R 180° about (3, 2). Draw and label the new triangle S.

(e) Rotate triangle S 90° anticlockwise about (0, 0). Draw and label the new triangle T. Write down the co-ordinates of each vertex (corner) of triangle T.

| **HWK 2M/2E** | **Main Book Page 210** |

In questions **1** and **2** copy each diagram. Use tracing paper to find the centre of each rotation.

1

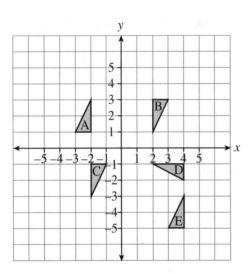

(a) rotation of ΔA onto ΔB

(b) rotation of ΔA onto ΔC

(c) rotation of ΔB onto ΔD

(d) rotation of ΔC onto ΔE

2 (a) rotation of shape P onto shape Q

(b) rotation of shape Q onto shape R

(c) rotation of shape Q onto shape S

(d) rotation of shape S onto shape T

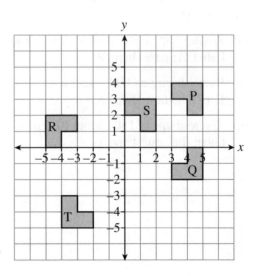

3 Draw axes with values from –8 to 8 and draw triangles with the following vertices:

triangle A: (–3, 3)   (–3, 6)   (–4, 3)

triangle B: (1, 3)   (1, 4)   (4, 3)

triangle C: (–3, 1)   (–4, 1)   (–3, –2)

triangle D: (1, –6)   (–2, –7)   (–2, –6)

triangle E: (2, –7)   (5, –7)   (5, –8)

triangle F: (3, 1)   (3, 4)   (4, 1)

Describe fully the following rotations or reflections.
For rotations give the angle, direction and centre. For reflections,
give the equation of the mirror line.

(a) triangle A ⟶ triangle B   (b) A ⟶ C

(c) C ⟶ D   (d) B ⟶ E   (e) B ⟶ F

HWK 3M ——————————————————————— **Main Book Page 212**

---

1 Copy this diagram.

(a) Translate triangle A
    6 units left and 1 unit down.
    Label the new triangle B.

(b) Rotate triangle B 180° about
    (–3, 0). Label the new triangle C.

(c) Reflect triangle C in the *y*-axis.
    Label the new triangle D.

(d) Translate triangle D 1 unit down.
    Label the new triangle E.

(e) What single transformation will
    move triangle E onto triangle A?

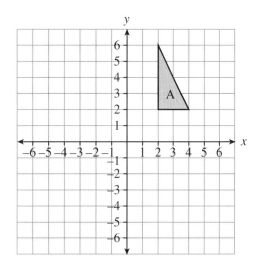

2 Copy this diagram.

(a) Rotate shape P 90° anticlockwise about (0, 0). Label the new shape Q.

(b) Reflect shape Q in the *y*-axis. Label the new shape R.

(c) Rotate shape R 90° anticlockwise about (1, –2). Label the new shape S.

(d) Reflect shape S in the *y*-axis. Label the new shape T.

(e) Describe the single translation which will move shape T onto shape P.

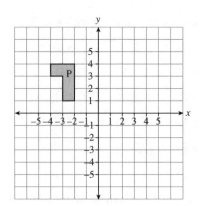

3

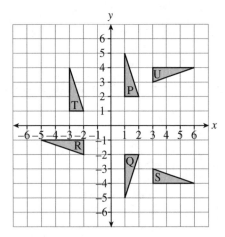

Describe fully the following transformations.

(a) triangle P onto triangle Q

(b) triangle Q onto triangle R

(c) triangle Q onto triangle S

(d) triangle P onto triangle T

(e) triangle P onto triangle U

(f) triangle S onto triangle U

HWK 3E ——————————————————————— **Main Book Page 214**

1 Triangle P can be transformed onto triangle Q by a combination of a rotation and a translation.

(a) Describe the rotation and the translation.

(b) Describe a different rotation and translation.

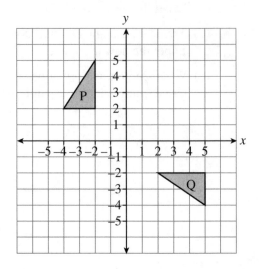

2

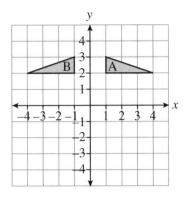

Describe the following transformations which will move triangle A onto triangle B.

(a) a reflection followed by a rotation

(b) a rotation followed by a reflection

(c) a reflection followed by a translation

(d) a translation followed by a reflection

3

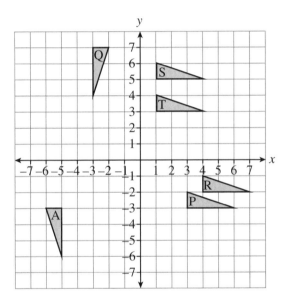

Triangle A can be transformed onto each of triangles P to T by a combination of a rotation and a reflection (in either order).

Describe the rotation and reflection for each triangle. (It may be helpful to copy the diagram first)

4   Draw a shape of your own on a set of axes. Move this shape with one transformation followed by another.

Challenge somebody in your next maths lesson to describe the two transformations you have used. (Your diagram should have just the original shape and the final shape)

4.7 Brackets and equations

HWK 1M ——————————————————— **Main Book Page 216**

In questions **1** to **6** answer true or false.

1 $3(x + 2) = 3x + 5$

2 $5(x - 4) = 5x - 20$

3 $2(4x + 3) = 14x$

4 $6(2x - 1) = 11x$

5 $4(2x + 7) = 8x + 28$

6 $3(2x - 1) = 6x - 3$

7 Copy and complete

(a) $4(3x - \square) = 12x - 8$

(b) $7(\square + 3p) = 42 + 21p$

(c) $3(\square - \square) = 15a - 24$

(d) $\square(4 + \square) = 20 + 35n$

In questions **8** to **19** remove the brackets and simplify.

8 $4(x + 3) + 2(x + 5)$

9 $5(x + 1) + 7(x + 3)$

10 $6(2x + 3) + 2(x + 7)$

11 $3(3x + 2) + 5(2x + 7)$

12 $4(3x + 1) + 3(5x + 2)$

13 $7(4x + 2) + 2(8x - 3)$

14 $6x + 3(2x - 1)$

15 $5(3x + 2) - 7x$

16 $4(2 + 5x) - 3x + 7$

17 $3 + 9(2x + 1) + 5x$

18 $3(4x + 3) - 4x + 2(x + 5)$

19 $6(3x - 2) - x + 4(2x + 3)$

20 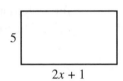 Write down an expression for the sum of the areas of these two rectangles. Simplify your answer.

3 $x + 4$ 5 $2x + 1$

21 Simplify $4(3x + 1) + 2(2x + 6) + 7(x + 8)$

22 Simplify $3(5x + 4) + 4(2 + 8x) + 8(2x + 5) + 2(1 + 7x)$

HWK 1E ──────────────────────── **Main Book Page 217**

In questions **1** to **6** answer true or false.

1 $-4(x + 3) = -4x + 3$

2 $-8(m - 2) = -8m - 16$

3 $-3(n + 2) = -3n - 6$

4 $-9(a - 3) = -9a + 27$

5 $-5(2 - y) = -10 + 5y$

6 $-2(4 + 3p) = -8 - 6p$

In questions **7** to **14** remove the brackets and simplify.

7 $3(x + 4) + 2(x - 3)$

8 $5(2x + 3) + 3(x - 2)$

9 $4(2x + 6) + 3(4x - 5)$

10 $5(3x + 4) - 4(2x - 3)$

11 $6(2x - 1) + 5(3x + 2)$

12 $7(2x + 3) - 5(x + 3)$

13 $8(4x + 7) - 4(3x + 8)$

14 $6(5x + 9) - 2(10x - 1)$

15 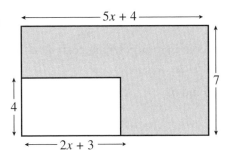 Write down an expression for the shaded area. Simplify your answer.

16 Copy and complete.

(a) $4(2x + 1) - \square\,(x - 3) = 3x + \square$

(b) $6(3x + 2) - \square\,(\square + 2) = 13x + 2$

In questions **17** to **19** remove the brackets and simplify.

17 $4(2a + 5b) - 5(a + 2b) + 3(3a - 4b)$

18 $7(5m + 6n) - 4(7m - 3n) - 5(m + 3n)$

19 $5(2x + 9y) - 6(x + 5y) + 3(4x + 7) - 4(2x - 1)$

HWK 2M	**Main Book Page 219**

Solve the equations.

1 $6a = 48$ **2** $4y - 15 = 21$ **3** $5p + 9 = 39$ **4** $8c - 17 = 15$

5 $6m - 30 = 42$ **6** $3n + 23 = 38$ **7** $4a + 16 = 36$ **8** $9y - 13 = 59$

9 $8x - 6 = 2$ **10** $6n - 85 = 35$ **11** $10m + 26 = 26$ **12** $60 = 7y + 39$

13 $4m = 2$ **14** $1 = 3y$ **15** $\frac{x}{4} = 2$

Now solve these:

16 $4x + 3 = 4$ **17** $7 + 4m = 10$ **18** $29 = 5y - 1$ **19** $6 = 4 + 3n$

20 $9a - 10 = 35$ **21** $6n + 14 = 14$ **22** $6p = 4p + 1$ **23** $17 = 5q - 7$

24 $10x + 3 = 8$

HWK 2E	**Main Book Page 220**

Solve the equations.

1 $3(n + 5) = 36$ **2** $6(n + 2) = 24$ **3** $8(n - 3) = 40$ **4** $7(2n - 3) = 49$

5 $4(2n + 1) = 36$ **6** $10(n - 6) = 30$ **7** $4(2n - 7) = 60$ **8** $6(5n + 2) = 42$

9 $2(n - 40) = 20$ **10** $4(n + 2) = 10$ **11** $12(2n - 1) = 4$ **12** $7(n + 4) = 33$

13   Dom has £n. He spends £20. He then looks at a £100 coat in a shop which costs five times the money he now has left.

     (a)   Write down an equation involving n.   (b)   Find n.

Now solve these:

14 $4(3n + 1) = 40$ **15** $30 = 2(n + 6)$ **16** $25 = 5(2n - 3)$

17 $90 = 3(n + 10)$ **18** $7(2n - 9) = 7$ **19** $120 = 8(n + 5)$

20 $15 = 4(2n + 3)$ **21** $6(4 + 5n) = 114$ **22** $2 = 3(5n - 1)$

HWK 3M	**Main Book Page 221**

In each question I am thinking of a number. Use the information to form an equation and then solve it to find the number.

1   If we multiply the number by 4 and then subtract 6, the answer is 50.

2   If we double the number and add 15, the answer is 53.

3   If we treble the number and subtract 16, the answer is 56.

4   If we multiply the number by 5 and then add 9, the answer is 74.

5   If we multiply the number by 8 and then add 12, the answer is 16.

6   If we double the number and subtract 5, the answer is 4.

In questions **7** to **14** form an equation with brackets and then solve it to find the number.

7   If we add 7 to the number and then double the result, the answer is 58.

8   If we subtract 15 from the number and then multiply the result by 3, the answer is 48.

9   If we subtract 14 from the number and then multiply the result by 6, the answer is 66.

10   If we double the number, add 1 and then multiply the result by 3, the answer is 117.

11   If we treble the number, subtract 7 and then multiply the result by 5, the answer is 445.

12   If we multiply the number by 4, subtract 13 and then multiply the result by 2, the answer is 18.

13   If we add 7 to the number and then multiply the result by 9, the answer is 65.

14   If we treble the number, subtract 8 and then multiply the result by 3, the answer is 12.

HWK 3E ──────────────────────────── **Main Book Page 222**

Solve the equations.

1 $6p + 10 = 4p + 16$

2 $7y - 3 = 4y + 18$

3 $4m + 7 = 2m + 11$

4 $10a - 12 = 5a + 18$

5 $6y - 32 = 2y + 28$

6 $8x + 13 = 6x + 23$

7 $10m + 14 = 6m + 66$

8 $5p - 27 = 2p + 33$

9 $2 + 5x = x + 42$

10 $9y - 12 = 3y$

11 $4n = 3n + 45$

12 $7p - 22 = 2p + 18$

13 $11 + 6a = 9a - 16$

14 $8m - 28 = m$

15

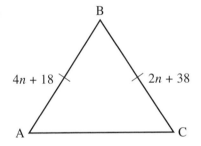

The sides AB and BC are equal.

Find the value of n then write down the length of side AB, assuming all values are in cm.

Solve these equations involving brackets.

16 $10(n + 4) = 9(n + 5)$

17 $6(n - 4) = 3(n + 2)$

18 $6(3n - 1) = 2(5n + 5)$

19 $8(n - 2) = 2(2n + 6)$

20 $15n + 6 = 3(4n + 3)$

21 $4(3n - 5) = 2(5n + 4)$

22 $7(n + 3) = 2(15 + 2n)$

23 $5(4 + 2n) = 2(3n + 10)$

24 $6n + 18 = 3(3n - 2)$

25 $5(4n - 2) = 3(12n - 6)$

HWK 4E ──────────────────────────── **Main Book Page 222**

Solve the equations.

1 $4(2x - 1) = 5(x + 2) - 2$

2 $53 + 3(p - 2) = 4(3p + 5)$

3 $2(3m + 1) + 16 = 6(2m - 3)$

4 $5(4a - 2) = 2(5a - 35)$

5 $7(2n + 5) = 3(3n - 15)$

6 $4y + 4 + 2y = 2(2y + 7)$

7 $9(2w - 7) = 12 + 3(5w + 2)$

8 $5(3x + 5) + 3 = 4(2x - 7)$

9 $7q + 3(2q - 1) = 8q + 17$

10 $33 + 8n = 5(4n - 3)$

Now solve these.

11 $2(9y - 7) = 4(3y + 2) - 4$

12 $16 + 20m = 8(3m - 5)$

13 $4(6x + 5) - 12x = 2(5x + 4)$

14 $7(3a - 2) = 7 + 6(2a + 7)$

15 $5(3n + 7) = 4(3n - 4) + 6$

16 $2 + 4(3p - 5) = 10(2p + 3)$

HWK 5M ──────────────────────── **Main Book Page 223**

1 This rectangle has an area of 120 cm². Form an equation and solve it to find x.

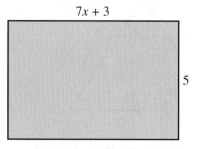

$7x + 3$

5

2 If I treble a number, take away 4 and then multiply the result by 3, the answer is 51. Find the number.

3

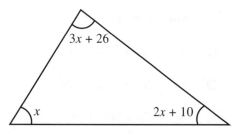

$3x + 26$

x

$2x + 10$

(a) Form an equation involving x.

(b) Solve the equation to find x.

(c) Write down the value of each angle in the triangle.

4 The sum of four consecutive numbers is 114. Find the four numbers.

5 PQ and QR are the equal sides in an isosceles triangle. Find the value of n.

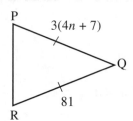

P

$3(4n + 7)$

Q

81

R

6 Alex has £($6n + 3$) and Fiona has £($3n + 15$). If they both have the same amount of money, form an equation involving n. Solve the equation and write down how much money Fiona has.

7 The perimeter of this rectangle is 38 cm.

(a) Form an equation involving x.

(b) Solve the equation to find x.

(c) Write down the values of the length and width of the rectangle.

$x + 2$

$3x + 1$

HWK 5E   **Main Book Page 224**

1 The angles in a quadrilateral are $x°$, $3x°$, $(2x + 15)°$ and $63°$. Find the angles in the quadrilateral.

2 Dave weighs ($5x + 3$)kg and Angie weighs ($4x + 7$)kg. They weigh a total of 136 kg. Find the value of x then write down how much each person weighs.

3

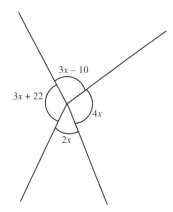

$3x - 10$

$3x + 22$

$4x$

$2x$

Form an equation involving x then use it to find the value of each angle shown.

4 The velocity v of a particle is given by the formula $v = u + at$.

Find the value of t if $u = 15$, $a = 10$ and $v = 105$.

5 The displacement s of a particle is given by the formula $s = ut + \frac{1}{2}at^2$.

Find the value of u if $a = 10$, $t = 6$ and $s = 228$.

6

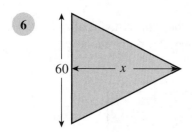

The triangle and the trapezium have the same area. Find x.

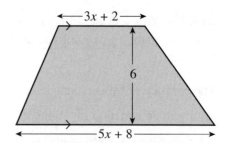

7

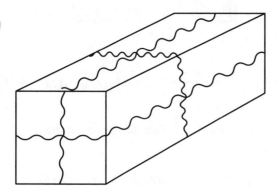

The length of a box is three time its width.
The height of the box is 2 cm more than its width.
String is wrapped around the box as shown by the wavy line.
10 cm is used for tying the string.
Find the length, width and height of the box if a total of 258 cm of string is used.

8   The sum of five consecutive *even* numbers is 240. Find the five numbers.

9   Gary scores x goals for his football team during one season. Wayne scores four times as many goals as Gary. Michael scores 7 goals more than Wayne and Steve scores 3 goals less than Wayne.

If the four players score a total of 69 goals between them, how many goals does each player score?

UNIT 5

5.1 Enlargement

1   Enlarge the two shapes shown by the scale factor given.

(a)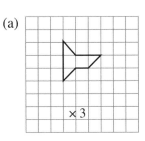

(b)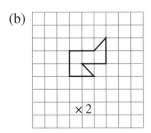

In questions **2** to **5**, look at each pair of diagrams and decide whether or not one diagram is an enlargement of the other. For each question write the scale factor of the enlargement or write 'not an enlargement'.

2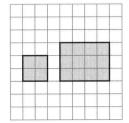

3

4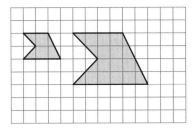

5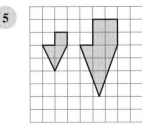

6   Is rectangle A an enlargement of rectangle B? *Explain* your answer.

3 cm — A — 8 cm   B — 12 cm, 4.5 cm

7   Is triangle Q an enlargement of triangle P? *Explain* your answer.

5 cm, P, 4 cm   12.5 cm, Q, 9 cm

8 Draw an enlargement of this picture with scale factor 2. Shade in the letters with different colours.

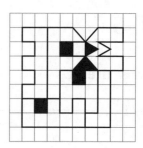

9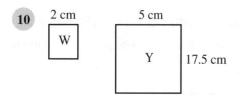

Triangle N is an enlargement of triangle M. Calculate the value of x.

10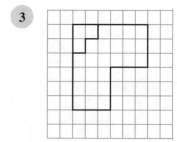

Rectangle Y is an enlargement of rectangle W. Calculate the area of rectangle W.

HWK 2M ─────────────────────────────── **Main Book Page 242**

Draw the shapes and then draw lines through corresponding points to find the centre of enlargement. Do not draw the shapes too near the edge of the page!

1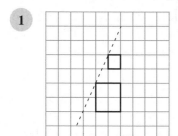

2

3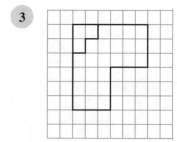

4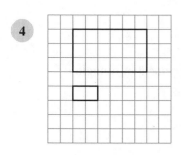

5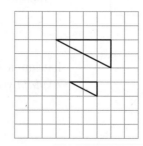

6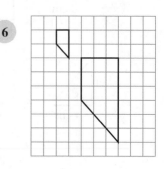

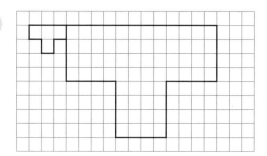

7

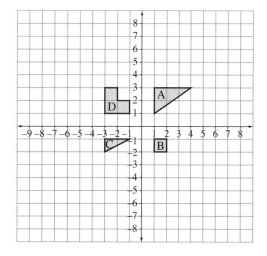

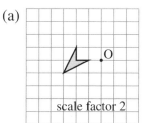

HWK 2E ——————————————————————————— **Main Book Page 243**

1 Copy each diagram and then draw an enlargement using the scale factor and centre of enlargement given.

(a) scale factor 2

(b) scale factor 2

2 (a) Copy this diagram.

(b) Enlarge shape A with scale factor 2 and centre of enlargement (0, 0).

(c) Enlarge shape B with scale factor 4 and centre of enlargement (0, 0).

(d) Enlarge shape C with scale factor 3 and centre of enlargement (0, 0).

(e) Enlarge shape D with scale factor 2 and centre of enlargement (0, 0).

3 (a) Draw an x axis from –8 to 8 and a y axis from –5 to 10. Draw triangle A with vertices at (1, 1), (1, 4) and (3, 1).

(b) Draw triangle B, the image of triangle A under enlargement with scale factor 3, centre (5, 1).

(c) Draw triangle C, the image of triangle A under enlargement with scale factor 2, centre (–1, 3).

(d) Draw triangle D, the image of triangle B under enlargement with scale factor $\frac{1}{3}$, centre (–4, –5).

(e) Draw triangle E, the image of triangle C under enlargement with scale factor $\frac{1}{2}$, centre (5, 9).

(f) Which triangles are congruent to triangle A?

(g) Write down the ratio of the area of triangle B to the area of triangle C in its simplest form.

5.2 Sequences and formulas

1 Copy and complete these mapping diagrams for finding sequence rules.

(a)

Term number (n)	$3n$	Term
1	→ 3 →	5
2	→ 6 →	8
3	→ 9 →	11
4	→ 12 →	14
⋮	⋮	⋮
10	→ ☐ →	☐
⋮	⋮	⋮
n	→ $3n$ →	$3n + 2$

(b)

Term number (n)	$6n$	Term
1	→ 6 →	7
2	→ 12 →	13
3	→ 18 →	19
4	→ 24 →	25
⋮	⋮	⋮
20	→ ☐ →	☐
⋮	⋮	⋮
n	→ ☐ →	☐

(c)

Term number (n)	$4n$	Term
1	→ 4 →	1
2	→ 8 →	5
3	→ 12 →	9
4	→ 16 →	13
⋮	⋮	⋮
25	→ ☐ →	☐
⋮	⋮	⋮
n	→ ☐ →	☐

(d)

Term number (n)	$2n$	Term
1	→ 2 →	8
2	→ 4 →	10
3	→ 6 →	12
4	→ 8 →	14
⋮	⋮	⋮
50	→ ☐ →	☐
⋮	⋮	⋮
n	→ ☐ →	☐

2 Here you are given the nth term. Copy and complete the diagrams.

(a)

Term number (n)	$5n$	Term
1	→ 5 →	12
2	→ ☐ →	☐
3	→ ☐ →	☐
4	→ ☐ →	☐
⋮	⋮	⋮
n	→ $5n$ →	$5n + 7$

(b)

Term number (n)	$6n$	Term
1	→ 6 →	2
2	→ ☐ →	☐
3	→ ☐ →	☐
4	→ ☐ →	☐
⋮	⋮	⋮
n	→ $6n$ →	$6n - 4$

(c)

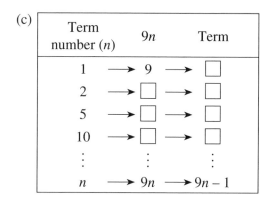

(d)

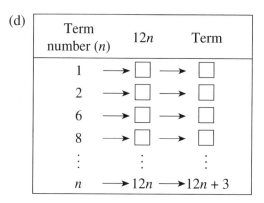

3 | $4n - 1$ | | $n + 4$ | | $2n$ | | $n - 1$ | | $3n + 2$ | | $4n$ |

Write down each sequence below and match it to the correct expression for the nth term shown above

(a) 4, 8, 12, 16, ...   (b) 3, 7, 11, 15, ...   (c) 0, 1, 2, 3, 4, ...   (d) 5, 8, 11, 14, 17, ...

4 Callum is on the beach collecting shells.

After 1 hour he has collected 15 shells.

After 2 hours he has 25 shells.

After 3 hours he has 35 shells.

After 4 hours he has 45 shells.

(a) How many shells do you expect him to have after 5 hours?

(b) Answer true or false. 'After n hours he will have $(15n + 10)$ shells'.

HWK 1E ———————————————————————— **Main Book Page 249**

> Remember: T(1) means 'the first term'
>
> T(2) means 'the second term'
>
> …. and so on.

1 For the sequence 5, 8, 11, 14, 17, ... write down

(a) T(3)   (b) T(5)   (c) T(10)

2 The nth term of a sequence is T(n) and T(n) = $4n - 1$.

Write down the values of:

(a) T(1)   (b) T(4)   (c) T(20)

3 The nth term of a sequence is T(n) and T(n) = $3n + 5$.

Find   (a) T(3)   (b) T(7)   (c) T(15)

4 Write the first five terms of the sequence where $T(n)$ is:

(a) $2n + 9$ (b) $3n - 6$ (c) $n^2 + 3$ (d) n^3

5 Copy and complete:

(a) 8, 11, 14, 17, … $T(n) = 3n + \boxed{}$

(b) 11, 13, 15, 17, … $T(n) = 2n + \boxed{}$

(c) 1, 6, 11, 16, … $T(n) = 5n - \boxed{}$

(d) 3, 13, 23, 33, … $T(n) = 10n - \boxed{}$

6 Find the nth term $T(n)$ for the sequence

6, 10, 14, 18, …

7 Find the nth term $T(n)$ for the sequence

3, 11, 19, 27, …

8 Find the value of n if:

(a) $T(n) = 4n - 3$ and $T(n) = 21$

(b) $T(n) = 5n + 4$ and $T(n) = 39$

(c) $T(n) = 12 - 5n$ and $T(n) = -8$

HWK 2M ———————————————————————— **Main Book Page 251**

1 Look at the sequence 5, 8, 11, 14, …

The *difference* between terms is 3.

Copy the table which has a column for $3n$.

Copy and complete:

'The nth term of the sequence is $3n + \boxed{}$.'

n	$3n$	term
1	3	5
2	6	8
3	9	11
4	12	14

2 Look at each sequence and the table underneath. Find the nth term in each case.

(a) Sequence 8, 13, 18, 23, …

n	$5n$	term
1	5	8
2	10	13
3	$\boxed{}$	18
4	$\boxed{}$	23

n^{th} term = $\boxed{}$

(b) Sequence 2, 6, 10, 14, …

n	$4n$	term
1	4	2
2	$\boxed{}$	6
3	$\boxed{}$	10
4	$\boxed{}$	14

n^{th} term = $\boxed{}$

3 Look at the sequence 5, 7, 9, 11, …

Write down the *difference* between terms.

Make a table like those in question **2** and use it to find the nth term.

4 Write down each sequence in a table and then find the nth term.

(a) 2, 8, 14, 20, … (b) 10, 13, 16, 19, … (c) 13, 22, 31, 40, …

5 Now find the nth term of these sequences.

(a) −19, −11, −3, 5, 13, … (b) 49, 43, 37, 31, 25, … (c) $1\frac{2}{3}, 2\frac{1}{3}, 3, 3\frac{2}{3}, …$

6 One fence panel has 4 vertical strips of wood.

Two fence panels joined together as shown have 7 vertical strips.

Three fence panels joined together are shown.

(a) How many vertical strips do 3 fence panels have?

(b) Draw four fence panels joined together.

(c) How many vertical strips do 4 fence panels have?

(d) How many vertical strips do 5 fence panels have?

(e) Copy and fill in the empty box:

'The number of vertical strips for n fence panels is $3n +$ ☐'

HWK 2E ——————————————————————— **Main Book Page 253**

In these questions you are given a sequence of shapes made from sticks or dots. If you need to, make a table to help you find the nth term of the sequence.

1 A pattern of sticks is made as shown below.

Shape number:	$n = 1$	$n = 2$	$n = 3$
Number of sticks:	4	7	10

Draw shape number 4 and shape number 5. How many sticks are there in the nth term?

2 Here is a pattern made with dots.

Shape number:	$n = 1$	$n = 2$	$n = 3$
Number of dots:	3	5	7

Draw the next diagram in the sequence. How many dots are there in the nth term?

3 Here is another pattern made with dots.

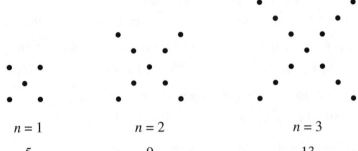

Shape number:	$n = 1$	$n = 2$	$n = 3$
Number of dots:	5	9	13

Draw the next diagram in the sequence. How many dots are there in the nth term?

4 Here is a sequence of hexagons made from sticks.

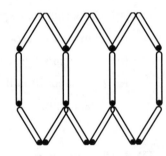

Shape number:	$n = 1$	$n = 2$	$n = 3$
Number of sticks:	6	11	16

Draw shape number 4. How many sticks are there in the nth term?

5 Here is another pattern made with dots.

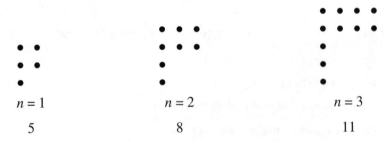

Shape number:	$n = 1$	$n = 2$	$n = 3$
Number of dots:	5	8	11

Draw the next diagram in the sequence. How many dots are there in the nth term?

6 Design your own sequence of shapes using sticks or dots which has an nth term equal to $2n + 6$.

5.3 Applying mathematics in a range of contexts 2

1

chocolates
£2.85 for 200 g

toffees
£2.15 for 150 g

Meryl buys 170 g of chocolates and 220 g of toffees.

Marston buys 225 g of chocolates and 170 g of toffees.

Who spends more and by how much?

2 Megan wants to enlarge photo A so that it will fit perfectly into frame B with no gaps around the edges. Find the height of frame B.

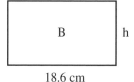

7.6 cm   A
12.4 cm

B   h
18.6 cm

3 Joshua buys 12 wooden posts each of length $2\frac{1}{5}$ m. He also buys 7 posts of length $1\frac{2}{3}$ m. What is the total weight of all 19 posts if one metre of this wood weighs 5.6 kg.

4 Ben has read five sevenths of his book. He has 90 pages left to read. How many pages are there in the book in total?

5

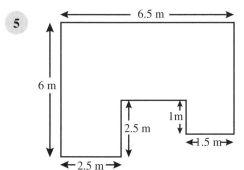

6.5 m

6 m

2.5 m

1 m

1.5 m

2.5 m

Amy tiles her kitchen floor with square tiles of side 50 cm. She buys the tiles in packs of 15. Each pack costs £37.60.

(a) How much will it cost to tile the floor?

(b) How many tiles will she have left over if she does not break any?

6 A 'Texas' shirt was £22 cheaper than a 'Winchester' shirt. The cost of each type of shirt is increased by £6 so that the cost of a 'Winchester' shirt is now double the cost of a 'Texas' shirt. What is the cost of a Winchester shirt now?

7 Simon and Kim drink a lot of tea and water when they are at work. Each day Simon drinks one more cup of tea than cups of water. Each day Kim drinks twice as many cups of tea as cups of water. They work for ten days during a fortnight and drink a total of 140 cups of tea and 90 cups of water. If they each drink the same number of cups of tea each day and the same number of cups of water each day, how many cups of tea does Simon drink each day and how many cups of tea does Kim drink each day?

8 A ball of radius 15 cm rolls down a hill. The ball makes 88 complete rotations. For how many metres does the ball roll? Give your answer to the nearest cm.

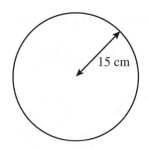

9

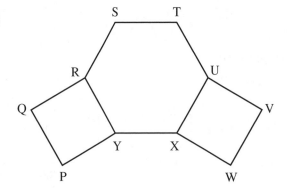

RSTUXY is a regular hexagon.
PQRY and UVWX are squares.
Find the value of PŶX.

5.4 Pythagoras' theorem

HWK 1M/1E ———————————————————— **Main Book Page 265**

Use Pythagoras' theorem in this exercise and give answers correct to 2 decimal places. The units are cm unless you are told otherwise.

1 Find the side marked with a letter.

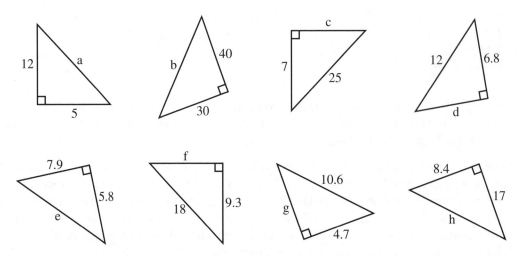

2

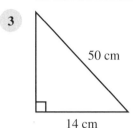

29 inches

14 inches

Calculate the length of the diagonal of this rectangular TV screen.

3

Calculate the area of this triangle.

50 cm

14 cm

4 A ladder of length 6 cm rests against a vertical wall, with its foot 2.3 m from the wall. Will the ladder reach a window which is 5.5 m above the ground? *Explain* your answer.

5 Find the value of *x* if this square has a diagonal of length 17 cm.

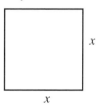

x

x

6 A balloon flies 25 miles north and then a further 18 miles west. How far is the balloon from its starting point?

7

8 cm

7 cm   7 cm

Calculate the area of this isosceles triangle.

HWK 2E ──────────────────────── **Main Book Page 269**

Give answers correct to 2 decimal places if necessary.

1 Find the length *x*. All lengths are in cm.

(a)

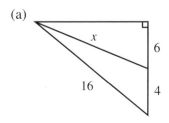

x

6

16

4

(b)

x

10

13

7.

(c)

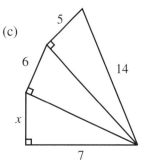

5

6

14

x

7

2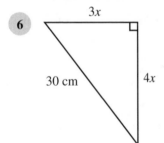

ABCD is a parallelogram. The area of a parallelogram is found using base × height
Calculate the area of ABCD.

B ← 9 cm → ← 5 cm → C

8 cm

A   D

3

B   C

A   D   3 cm

Q ⋯⋯⋯⋯⋯ R

6 cm

P   S

9 cm

(a) Use triangle PQS to find the length of QS.

(b) Use triangle BSQ to find the length of BS.

4 Find the length of the diagonal XY in the cuboid opposite.

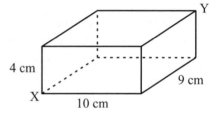

Y

4 cm   9 cm

X

10 cm

5 Find the length of the longest pencil which would fit into a rectangular box measuring 15 cm × 9 cm × 4 cm.

6

3x

30 cm   4x

Calculate the value of x.

5.5 Drawing and using graphs

| HWK 1M/1E | Main Book Page 272 |

For each question, complete a table then draw the graph using the scales given.

1 $y = 2x + 2$ for x-values from 0 to 5

2x + 2 means [x] → [×2] → [+2]

x	0	1	2	3	4	5
y					10	
coordinates					(4, 10)	

(x-axis: use 1 cm for 1 unit
y-axis: use 1 cm for 2 units)

2 $y = 3x + 1$ for x-values from 0 to 5

$3x + 1$ means $\boxed{x} \longmapsto \boxed{\times 3} \longmapsto \boxed{+1}$

(x-axis: 1 cm for 1 unit, y-axis: 1 cm for 2 units)

3 $y = \frac{1}{2}x + 2$ for x-values from 0 to 6

$\frac{1}{2}x + 2$ means $\boxed{x} \longmapsto \boxed{\times \frac{1}{2}} \longmapsto \boxed{+2}$

(x-axis: 1 cm for 1 unit, 2 cm for 1 unit)

4 Draw $3x + y = 6$; take x values from 0 to 4.

5 On the same graph, draw the lines
$$y = 1.5x - 4$$
$$y = \frac{1}{6}x$$
$$x + 2y = 8$$

Take x-values from 0 to 8. Write down the coordinates of the three vertices of the triangle formed.

HWK 2M ———————————————— **Main Book Page 275**

1 Using the same axes, draw the graphs of $y = 3x - 1$, $y = 3x - 3$, $y = 3x$ and $y = 3x + 3$.
Write down what you notice about each line and its equation.
(Clues: where do the lines cut the y-axis? – are the lines parallel?)

2 Three of the lines below are parallel. Write down the equation of the line which is *not* parallel to the other lines.

$\boxed{y = 4x + 1}$ $\boxed{y = 3x + 4}$ $\boxed{y = 4x - 2}$ $\boxed{y = 4x + 4}$

3 Draw the graph of $y = x^2 + 2$ using x-values from 0 to 4.

4 State which of the following represent straight line graphs:

$\boxed{y = x^2 - 3}$ $\boxed{y = 4x + 2}$ $\boxed{y = 5x - 3}$ $\boxed{y = 3x^2}$

5 Write down the coordinates of the point where $y = 5x - 7$ cuts the y-axis.

6 Write down the equations of 3 lines which would make a diagram like the one shown opposite.

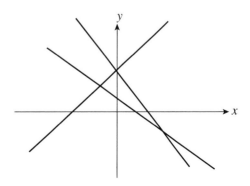

HWK 2E ———————————————————— **Main Book Page 276**

In questions ① to ⑩ you are given the coordinates of several points on a line. Find the equation of each line.

1

x	1	2	3	4	5
y	5	6	7	8	9

2

x	1	2	3	4	5
y	5	10	15	20	25

3

x	10	12	14	16	18
y	4	6	8	10	12

4

x	20	19	18	17	16
y	0	1	2	3	4

5

x	2	4	6	8	10
y	16	32	48	64	80

6

x	1	2	3	4	5
y	1	3	5	7	9

7

x	1	2	3	4	5
y	5	7	9	11	13

8

x	1	2	3	4	5
y	2	5	8	11	14

9

x	1	2	3	4	5
y	7	12	17	22	27

10

x	1	2	3	4	5
y	11	13	15	17	19

11

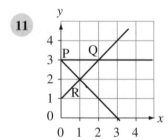

Find the equation of the line through

(a) R and Q   (b) P and Q   (c) P and R

12

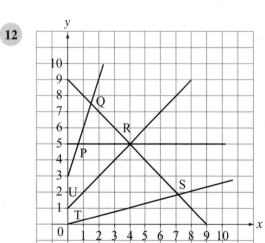

Find the equation of the line through

(a) P and R   (b) U and R

(c) T and S   (d) Q and S

(e) P and Q

HWK 3E ———————————————————— **Main Book Page 278**

Draw the graph for each equation in questions ① to ④ .

1 $y = x^2 + 4$ for x values from –3 to +3.

2 $y = x^2 + 2x$ for x values from –3 to +3.

3 $y = (x - 1)^2$ for x values from –2 to +4.

4 $y = x^2 - 6x + 9$ for x values from 0 to 6.

5   Draw the graphs of $y = (x + 2)^2$ and $y = x + 3$ for values of x from –4 to +1. Write down the x coordinates, correct to 1 decimal place, of the two points where the line cuts the curve.

HWK 4M ———————————————————— **Main Book Page 279**

1   One gallon is approximately 4.5 litres.

    (a) Draw axes, as shown, with a scale of 1 cm for 1 gallon and 1 cm for 5 litres. Draw a 'x' where 45 litres are equal to 10 gallons. Draw another 'x' at (0, 0).

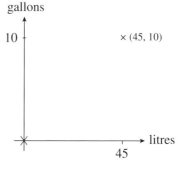

    (b) Draw a long straight line through the two points above and use your graph to convert:

       (i) 2 gallons into litres   (ii) 37.5 litres into gallons

    (c) Ben puts 13.5 litres of petrol into his car. This costs him £15.45. Use your graph to help you calculate the cost of 1 gallon of petrol.

2   A man climbing a mountain measures his height above sea level after every 30 minutes; the results are shown below.

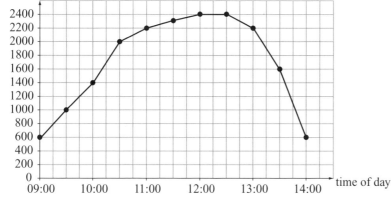

height above sea level (m)

    (a) At what height was he at 10:00 h?

    (b) At what height was he at 13:30 h?

    (c) Estimate his height above sea level at 09:45 h.

    (d) Estimate his altitude at 10:45 h.

    (e) Estimate his height above sea level at 13:45 h.

    (f) At what two times was he 2200 m above sea level?

    (g) How high was the mountain? (He got to the top!)

    (h) How long did he rest at the summit?

    (i) How long did he take to reach the summit?

3 Two tool hire firms charge the following amounts for the hire of a large tile cutter.

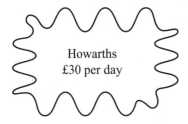

Howarths
£30 per day

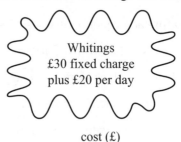

Whitings
£30 fixed charge
plus £20 per day

(a) Draw axes for the number of days hired and the cost.

(b) Use the axes to draw a graph for each tool hire firm to show the cost for up to 5 days.

(c) Which tool hire firm is the cheaper to use for 4 days?

(d) For how many days hire do both firms charge the same amount?

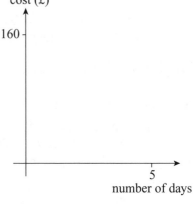

cost (£)

160

5
number of days

5.6 Using ratios

HWK 1M ——————————————————— **Main Book Page 281**

1 30:18 is the same as 5:3 because both numbers can be divided by 6.

Write these ratios in a more simple form.

(a) 32:12   (b) 20:120   (c) 15:40   (d) 12:18:36

(e) 21:35   (f) 54:36   (g) 28:16:32   (h) 18:45:27

2 There are 90 boys and 70 girls on the school field. Write down the ratio of boys to girls in its simplest form.

3 The Carlton family have three times as many rabbits as dogs. Write down the ratio of rabbits to dogs.

4 The ratio of men to women in a drama group is 5:3. If there are 20 men, how many women are there?

5 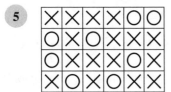 Write down the ratio of noughts to crosses in its simplest form.

6 Charlie has cartons of juice in a large box. The ratio of orange to apple is 3:4. If Charlie has 18 cartons of orange juice, how many cartons of apple juice does he have?

7 Toni has some felt tip pens. The colours red to blue to green are in the ratio 5:2:3. If Toni has 12 green pens, how many red pens does she have and how many blue pens does she have?

8 Margaret and Kelly go out on their bikes one day. The ratio of the distances they travel is 7:12. Kelly travels the furthest. If Kelly travels 36 km, how far does Margaret travel?

9 If $\frac{3}{7}$ of the animals in a vet's surgery are cats and the rest are dogs, what is the ratio of cats to dogs?

10 The ratio of boys to girls in a class is 4:5. What fraction of the class are boys?

HWK 1E ——————————————————————— **Main Book Page 283**

1 Nick and Beth share a bag of 32 toffees in the ratio 3:5. How many toffees does each person get?

2 Some red and blue paint is mixed together in the ratio 7:2. If 27 litres of paint is used in total, how much of each colour paint is used?

3 Share each quantity in the ratio given.

(a) £800, 3:7   (b) £144, 7:5   (c) £1500, 3:1:6

4 In Jennifer's workshop, the ratio of nails to screws is 9:5. If there are 450 screws, how many nails are there?

5 The angles in a triangle are in the ratio 4:3:2. Find the size of the largest angle.

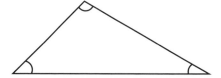

6 Find the smallest share in each of these problems.

(a) £48, ratio 5:11   (b) 320 kg, ratio 5:2:3

7 The marks in an exam are given for three different parts in the ratio 11:5:4. The maximum mark for the exam is 100. Write down the maximum marks which can be awarded for each part of the exam.

8 Hugo and Ellie's mother gives them £80 in the ratio 7:9. Hugo gets the smallest share. Hugo owes Ellie £15 and so he gives her this money. Write down the ratio of Hugo's money to Ellie's money now. Write the ratio in its simplest form.

9

Find

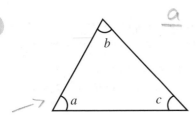

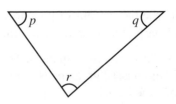

Angles in the triangle above are in the ratio 5:4:3. Angle b is the middle sized angle.

here is a

Angles in the triangle above are in the ratio 3:1:5. Angle p is the middle sized angle. Angle r is the largest angle.

Find the size of angle r if angle p is equal in size to angle b.

HWK 2E — **Main Book Page 284**

1 The sides of a rectangle are in the ratio 7:3. The perimeter of the rectangle is 40 cm. Find the area of the rectangle.

2 The ratio of Wayne's weight to Caroline's weight is 3:2. How much does Wayne weigh if he weighs 20 kg more than Caroline?

3 The ratio of children to adults in a room is 2:5. Amongst the adults the ratio of men to women is 3:4. Find the ratio of children to men.

4

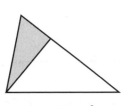

area = 21 cm²

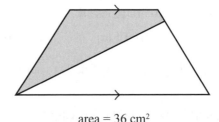

area = 36 cm²

The shaded area to the unshaded area in the triangle is in the ratio 1:2. The shaded area to the unshaded area in the trapezium is in the ratio 4:5. Find the ratio of the total shaded area to the total unshaded area.

5 Find y if $y:20 = 5:y$

6 A rectangular photo measures 18 cm by 7 cm. The lengths are enlarged in the ratio 2:3. What is the ratio of the area of the original photo to the area of the enlarged photo?

7 Beer and lemonade is mixed in the ratio 3:2 to make a shandy. 5% of the beer is alcohol. What percentage of the shandy is alcohol?

8 The ratio $m:n = 2:7$ and the ratio $n:p = 3:5$. Find the ratio $m:p$.

1 The scale of a map is 1:100 000. The distance between 2 towns on a map is 8 cm. What is the actual distance in kilometres between the two towns?

2 Find the actual distance in metres between two pylons which are 2 cm apart on a map whose scale is 1:10 000.

3 The length of a field on a map is 1.5 cm. Find the actual length of the field if the map scale is 1:40 000.

4 Two cities are 6.5 cm apart on a map and the scale of the map is 1:2 000 000. What is the actual distance between the two cities?

5 A map has a scale of 1:50 000. The distance from Tom's house to the 'Red Bull' pub is 3 cm and the distance from Tom's house to the 'White Horse' pub is 5.5 cm. How many kilometres further from Tom's house is the White Horse than the Red Bull?

6 Colin and Adele are hiking. They fix their positions and are 12 km from each other. How far is this on a map if the scale is 1:200 000?

7 Two ships are 30 km apart from each other. How far is this on a map if the scale is 1:50 000?

8 Map A has a scale of 1:200 000. Map B has a scale of 1:50 000. Two villages are 8 cm apart on map A. How far apart will the two villages be on map B?

9 Bristol and Wells are 16 cm apart on map A with a scale of 1:200 000. How far apart would they be on map B with a scale of 1:500 000?

10 (a) The area of a lake on a map is 18 cm². Work out the actual area of the lake if the scale of the map is 1:40 000. (Be careful!)

    (b) What is the area of the same lake on a map with a scale of 1:50 000?

5.7 Congruent shapes, tessellation

1 Decide which shapes are congruent pairs. (You can use tracing paper)

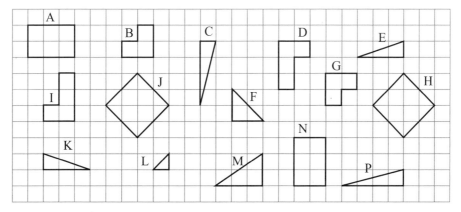

2 Draw a pentagon (5 sided shape) then draw a congruent pentagon.

3 Draw a hexagon (6 sided shape) then draw a congruent hexagon.

4

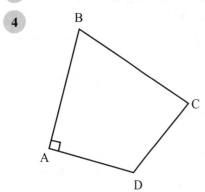 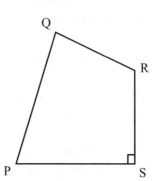

The two shapes above are congruent. Sam says that side AD is equal to side SR.
Is Sam correct?

5 Draw and colour a design which uses at least 3 different types of congruent shape.

| **HWK 2M** | **Main Book Page 290** |

1 Draw any quadrilateral (4 sided shape) on paper or card and cut it out. Use this template to draw a tessellation and colour in this pattern.

2 Draw another tessellation pattern using *at least* two different shapes. Colour in this pattern. An example is shown opposite.

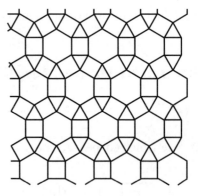

UNIT 6

6.1 More Algebra

HWK 1M **Main Book Page 302**

Solve the equations.

1 $5x - 3 = 17$ **2** $7 + 4x = 35$ **3** $86 = 9x - 4$ **4** $44 = 12 + 8x$

5 $19 = 7n - 16$ **6** $4 = 7x + 3$ **7** $9x - 4 = 3$ **8** $3x - 2 = -4$

9 $7 = 2x + 15$ **10** $5 - x = 11$ **11** $5 = 20 - 3x$ **12** $1 = 2 + 6x$

Now solve these equations.

13 $8x - 6 = 6x + 2$ **14** $4x + 27 = 2x + 45$ **15** $5x + 45 = 9x - 15$

16 $5x - 16 = 2x + 14$ **17** $7x + 33 = 54 + 4x$ **18** $4x - 3 = 1 - x$

19 $7x + 4 = 2 - 4x$ **20** $8 - 3x = 3 + 3x$ **21** $5 - 2x = 6x - 2$

22 $3 - 2x = 5x + 17$ **23** $9x + 8 = 18 + 11x$ **24** $6 - 4x = 3 - 6x$

HWK 1E **Main Book Page 303**

Solve the equations.

1 $\frac{x}{4} = 6$ **2** $7 = \frac{x}{5}$ **3** $-3 = \frac{x}{7}$ **4** $\frac{4x}{5} = 8$

5 $\frac{x}{6} = -9$ **6** $1 = \frac{5x}{3}$ **7** $\frac{3x}{4} = -2$ **8** $\frac{2}{x} = 9$

9 $7 = \frac{5}{x}$ **10** $\frac{6}{x} = \frac{3}{4}$ **11** $-4 = \frac{3}{x}$ **12** $\frac{20}{x} = -13$

Now solve these equations.

13 $\frac{x}{2} + 4 = 6$ **14** $7 + \frac{x}{4} = 10$ **15** $\frac{x}{7} - 3 = 3$ **16** $\frac{5x}{6} - 1 = 0$

17 $\frac{2x}{5} + 3 = 4$ **18** $\frac{1x}{4} - 9 = 2$ **19** $5 - \frac{x}{3} = 2$ **20** $7 + \frac{3x}{4} = 13$

21 $\frac{5}{x} - 3 = 4$ **22** $\frac{6}{x} + 5 = 4$ **23** $10 - \frac{4}{x} = 13$ **24** $\frac{4}{3x} + 6 = 1$

HWK 2M **Main Book Page 304**

Solve the equations.

1 $5(x + 3) = 2(2x + 11)$ **2** $7(x + 6) = 11(2x - 3)$ **3** $4(2x - 3) = 3(2 + 2x)$

4 $3(4x + 1) = 9(2x - 1)$ **5** $8(2x - 7) = 2x$ **6** $6(x + 9) = 3(8 + 3x)$

7   $3(3x + 5) = 29(x - 5)$ 8 $10(9 + 2x) = 33(x - 2)$ 9 $4(2x + 1) - 2(x + 4) = 0$

10 $5(x - 4) - 2 = 3(3 - x)$ 11 $6(2x + 3) - (3x + 2) = 0$ 12 $5 + 2(4x + 3) = 6$

13 $3(2x + 5) + 2(3 - x) = 5x$ 14 $8x - 3(x - 3) = 2x$ 15 $3x - 4(2x + 5) = 2x$

HWK 2E ──────────────────────────────────── **Main Book Page 305**

In each question, I am thinking of a number. Use the information to form an equation and then solve it to find the number.

1   If I subtract 3 from the number and then multiply the result by 6, the answer is 14.

2   If I treble the number and then add 5, the answer is 3.

3   If I double the answer, subtract 5 and then treble the result, the answer is 6.

4   If I multiply the number by 5, add 2 and then double the result, the answer is 7.

5   If I multiply the number by 6 and subtract 7, I get the same answer as when I add 4 to the number and then treble the result.

6   If I add 3 to the number and then multiply the result by 5, I get the same answer as when I subtract 2 from the number and then treble the result.

7   If I treble the number, subtract 2 and then multiply the result by 4, the answer I get is the same as when I treble the number and add 14.

8   If I multiply the number by 4, add 1 and then multiply the result by 5, the answer I get is the same as when I double the number and subtract 4.

9   If I subtract the number *from* 4 and then multiply the result by 3, I get the same answer as when I add 3 to the number and then multiply the result by 7.

10 If I treble the number, add 7 and then divide the result by 2, I get the same answer as when I subtract the number *from* 3 and then treble the result.

HWK 3M/3E ──────────────────────────────────── **Main Book Page 306**

1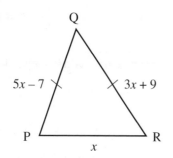

PQ = QR in this isosceles triangle.

All measurements are in cm.

(a) Find x

(b) Find the perimeter of the triangle.

2 Football shorts cost £$2x$ and football shirts cost £$(3x + 2)$. Two pairs of shorts and three shirts cost £162 in total. Find the cost of one shirt.

3 Maurice is 40 years younger than his father. In 15 years time his father will be three times as old as Maurice. How old is Maurice now?

4

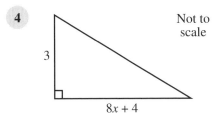

Not to scale

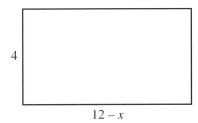

The area of the triangle is twice the area of the rectangle. Find the area of the triangle. All lengths are in cm.

5 The sum of five consecutive whole numbers is 355. Find the five numbers.

6 Rachel delivers newspapers each day. She starts with 81 newspapers. She delivers $2x$ newspapers on Stanley Street and $(x - 3)$ papers on Cumberland Drive. She then has x newspapers remaining. How many newspapers did she deliver on Cumberland Drive?

7

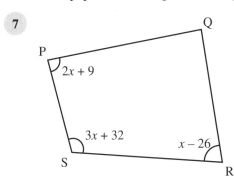

Angle Q is the difference between angles S and P. Find the values of the four angles in this quadrilateral.

8

The perimeter of this isosceles triangle is $(8x + 5)$ cm.

Find the value of the perimeter if one of the equal sides is 25 cm long.

9 In this number wall the number in each brick is found by adding the numbers in the two bricks below. Find the value of n.

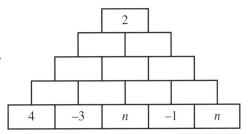

6.2 Volume of objects

1

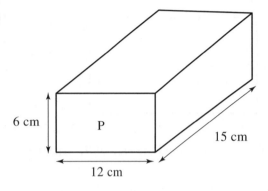

Which cuboid has the larger volume and by how much?

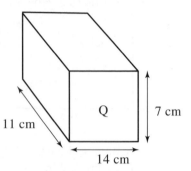

2 Find the volume of this solid by splitting it into three cuboids. All lengths are in cm.

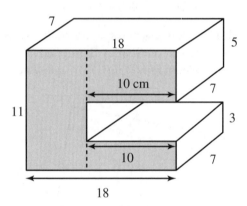

3

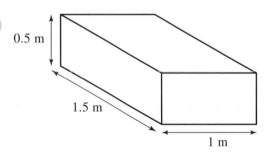

This water tank is full of water.
Hannah uses 0.32 m³ of water.
What volume of water is left in the tank?

4 The entrance to a 300 m tunnel is shown opposite.
Work out the volume of the tunnel.

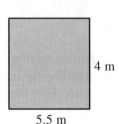

4 m

5.5 m

5 Find the length *x* for each cuboid.

(a)

3 cm
x
6 cm
volume = 90 cm³

(b)

9 m
15 m
x
volume = 810 m³

(c)

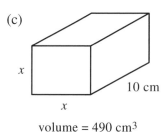

x
10 cm
x
volume = 490 cm³

6

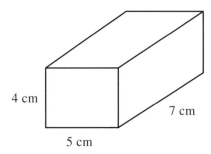

4 cm
7 cm
5 cm

(a) Draw a *net* for this cuboid.

(b) Work out the volume of this cuboid.

(c) Work out the total surface area of this cuboid.

7   2 m

5 m

3 m

The container on a lorry is shown opposite.

Sand is tipped into the lorry at a rate of 0.2 m³ per minute.

How long does it take to completely fill the container with sand?

8 How many small cubes of side 0.1 m will fit into a large cube of side 2.4 m?

9 (a) Write down an expression for the volume of this cuboid.

(b) Write down an expression for the total surface area of the cuboid.

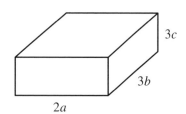

3c
3b
2a

10 (a) Write down an expression for the difference in the volumes of these two cuboids.

(b) Write down an expression for the difference in the total surface areas of these two cuboids.

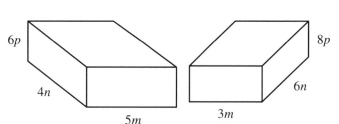

6p
4n
5m

8p
6n
3m

110

> Reminder: volume of a prism = (area of cross section) × (length)

Find the volume of each prism.

1

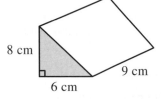

8 cm

9 cm

6 cm

2

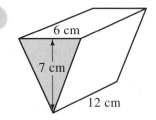

6 cm

7 cm

12 cm

3

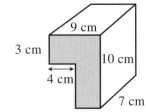

9 cm

3 cm

10 cm

4 cm

7 cm

4

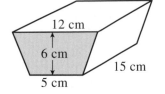

12 cm

6 cm

15 cm

5 cm

5

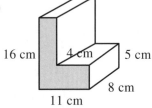

16 cm

4 cm   5 cm

8 cm

11 cm

6

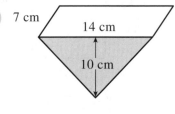

7 cm

14 cm

10 cm

7

prism A

Which prism
has the larger
volume and by
how much?

prism B

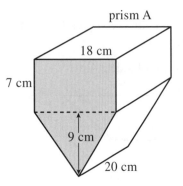

18 cm

7 cm

9 cm

20 cm

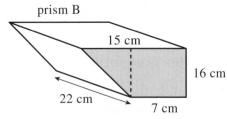

15 cm

16 cm

22 cm

7 cm

1 Find the capacity, in litres, of a rectangular oil tank with internal dimensions 70 cm by 25 cm by 1.2 m. (1 litre = 1000 cm³)

2

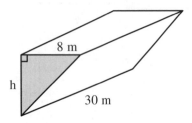

8 m

h

30 m

Find the height h of this triangular prism if the volume is 2160 m³.

3

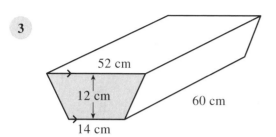

This container is full of water. The water leaks out of a hole in the bottom at a rate of 30 ml/sec. How long will it take for the container to become empty? (1 ml = 1 cm³)

4 The front of this bridge is a semicircle cut from a rectangle. 1 m³ of the stone used to make the bridge weighs 1150 kg. Calculate the weight of the stone used to make the complete bridge. (give your answer to the nearest kg)

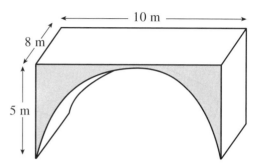

5

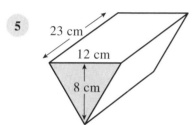

These two prisms have the same volumes. Find the value of x.

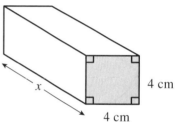

6

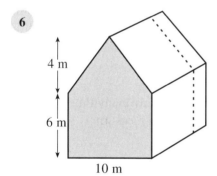

John owns a house with a volume of 1280 m³. He wants to extend the house backwards using the entire cross section so that the volume of the house increases by 15%. How far will he extend the house backwards?

HWK 3M — **Main Book Page 318**

Give answers correct to 3 significant figures where necessary.

1 Find the volume of a cylinder of radius 4 cm and length 9 cm.

2 Find the volume of each prism.

(a)

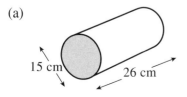

(b)

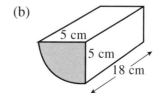

3 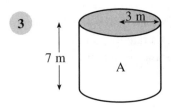 Which cylinder has the larger volume and by how much?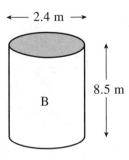

4 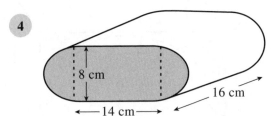 Calculate the volume of this prism.

5 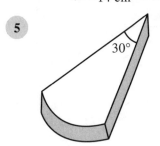 This slice of pie is cut from a circular pie of diameter 20 cm and thickness 5 cm. Calculate the volume of this slice.

HWK 3E ———————————————————— **Main Book Page 319**

Give answers correct to 3 significant figures where necessary.

1 A cylindrical glass has a diameter of 7.5 cm and a height of 10 cm. How many times can the glass be filled completely with juice from a rectangular carton measuring 21 cm × 13 cm × 8 cm?

2  A rubber washer has an outside diameter of 18 mm and an inside diameter of 12 mm. Calculate the volume of the washer if its thickness is 3 mm.

3 Calculate the radius of a cylinder of height 12 cm which has a volume of 1550 cm³.

4 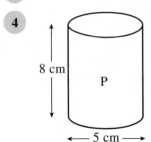 The cylinder is full of milk. All the milk is poured into the rectangular metal box. How far from the top of the box does the milk go up to?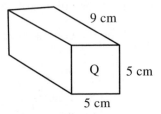

5 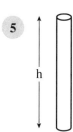 A 4 cm × 4 cm × 2 cm slab of chocolate is melted then made into twenty thin cylindrical chocolate sticks of diameter 4 mm. If 10% of the chocolate is wasted during the process, what is the length of one chocolate stick?

6 This rectangular piece of paper wraps perfectly around a tin can with no gaps at the top or bottom. Calculate the volume of the can.

20 cm

7 cm

6.3 Percentages 2

HWK 1M ———————————————————— **Main Book Page 322**

(a) Start in the top left box.

(b) Change the number to a fraction, decimal or % as required.

(c) Find this answer in the top corner of another box.

(d) Write down the letter in that box.

(e) Repeat steps (b), (c) and (d) until you arrive at the top left box.

(f) Write down the message.

$\frac{7}{20}$ D $(2-1.86) \rightarrow \%$	28% R $(\frac{1}{2}-0.48) \rightarrow$ decimal	37.5% K $\frac{3}{8} \rightarrow$ decimal	0.095 U $(20\%$ of $16) \rightarrow$ decimal
0.375 E $(10\%$ of $2.5) \rightarrow$ decimal	22.5% G $(10\%$ of $0.1) \rightarrow$ decimal	14% M $\frac{4}{25} \rightarrow$ decimal	38% W $22\% \rightarrow$ fraction

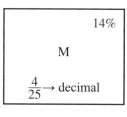

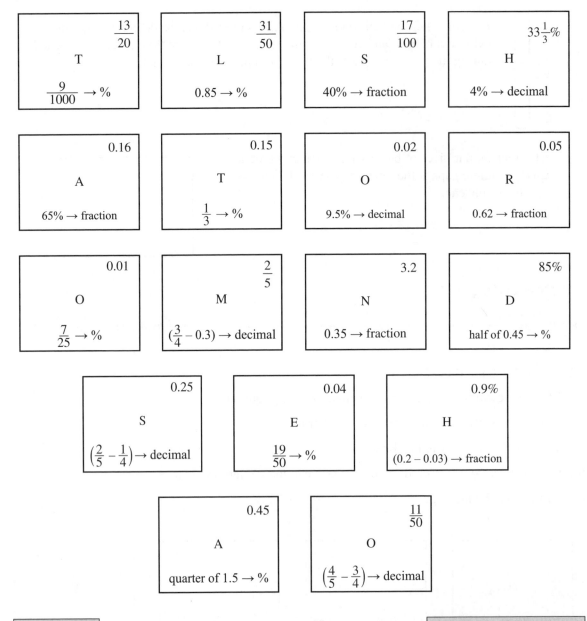

$\dfrac{13}{20}$ T $\dfrac{9}{1000} \rightarrow \%$	$\dfrac{31}{50}$ L $0.85 \rightarrow \%$	$\dfrac{17}{100}$ S $40\% \rightarrow$ fraction	$33\dfrac{1}{3}\%$ H $4\% \rightarrow$ decimal
0.16 A $65\% \rightarrow$ fraction	0.15 T $\dfrac{1}{3} \rightarrow \%$	0.02 O $9.5\% \rightarrow$ decimal	0.05 R $0.62 \rightarrow$ fraction
0.01 O $\dfrac{7}{25} \rightarrow \%$	$\dfrac{2}{5}$ M $\left(\dfrac{3}{4} - 0.3\right) \rightarrow$ decimal	3.2 N $0.35 \rightarrow$ fraction	85% D half of $0.45 \rightarrow \%$

0.25 S $\left(\dfrac{2}{5} - \dfrac{1}{4}\right) \rightarrow$ decimal	0.04 E $\dfrac{19}{50} \rightarrow \%$	0.9% H $(0.2 - 0.03) \rightarrow$ fraction

0.45 A quarter of $1.5 \rightarrow \%$	$\dfrac{11}{50}$ O $\left(\dfrac{4}{5} - \dfrac{3}{4}\right) \rightarrow$ decimal

HWK 2M ———————————————————————————— **Main Book Page 323**

You may use a calculator. Give all answers to one decimal place.

1 8 people out of 15 in a rugby team are more than 6 feet tall. What percentage of the team are more than 6 feet tall?

2 ☺ ☹ ☺   What percentage of these faces are 'smiley'?
☹ ☺ ☺
☺ ☺ ☺

3 17 out of 163 people thought that 'Little Britain' was the best comedy programme ever. What percentage of the people was this?

4 A 150 g chocolate bar contains 59 g fat and 12 g fibre. What percentage of the chocolate bar is *not* fat or fibre?

5 The table shows how many children wear glasses in Year 8 at Denton High School.

(a) What percentage of the girls wear glasses?

(b) What percentage of all the children do not wear glasses?

	Boys	Girls	Total
wear glasses	17	28	45
do not wear glasses	74	102	176
Total	91	130	221

6 Work out the following, giving each answer correct to the nearest penny.

(a) 3.2% of £39 (b) 6.5% of £73 (c) 3.9% of £16.80

7 Increase £52.46 by 7.3%. Give your answer correct to the nearest penny.

8 Three basketball players are shooting baskets. Their success rate is shown opposite.

(a) Who had the highest percentage rate of success?

(b) What was the percentage difference in success rates between Cheryl and Mike?

	successes	total attempts
Jason	39	143
Cheryl	48	170
Mike	27	71

9

	Men	Women	Total
under 21	174	263	437
21 to 65	320	419	739
over 65	211	306	517
Total	705	988	1693

One day a supermarket records the ages of the shoppers. This information is shown in the table.

(a) What percentage of the men were over 65?

(b) What percentage of the people were 21 to 65 years old?

(c) What percentage of the women were 65 or *under* 65 years old?

HWK 2E ———————————————————— **Main Book Page 325**

In questions 1 to 4 multiply by a single decimal to find each answer.

1 (a) Increase £720 by 9%. (ie. work out 720 × 1.09)

(b) Increase 930 kg by 4%.

(c) Decrease 4700 m by 3.5%.

2 A bus fare of £6 is increased by 6%. What is the new bus fare?

3 A farmer owns 530 hectares of land. The farmer sells 32% of his land. What is the area of land that he now owns?

4 A rock star sells 1360 000 albums during one year. Sales increase by 17% during the following year. How many albums does the rock star sell during the following year?

5 $p = \dfrac{a}{b^3}$

(a) Calculate, to 3 s.f., the value of p when $a = 510$ and $b = 4$.

(b) Calculate the new value of p if a is increased by 12% and b is decreased by 28%.

6

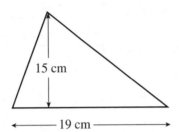

(a) Find the difference between the area of the triangle and the area of the circle.

(b) The diameter of the circle is increased by 14%. The height of the triangle is increased by 20% and the base of the triangle is decreased by 6%. Find the difference now between the area of the triangle and the area of the circle.

7 A company makes kitchen units. In one year, production costs are £784 000 and transport costs are £329 000.

45% of production costs are for raw materials and the remainder are machine costs. In the following year, the cost of raw materials rises by 18%, machine costs increase by 7% and transport costs rise by 14%.

What is the overall increase in costs for this company during the following year?

8

Week 1
All prices increase by 8%

Week 7
All prices decrease by 8%

A shop increases all its prices in week 1 then, due to poor sales, decreases the prices in week 7. A jacket costs £76 at the start of week 1. How much will the jacket cost at the end of week 7?

9 Paula's car is worth £7000. One year later it loses 14% of its value.

(a) How much is the car worth now?

(b) It loses 14% of this new value during the following year. How much is the car worth at the end of that year?

10

4%

Terry invests £5000 in a building society for 4 years. Each year his money makes 4% interest on the amount in his account at the start of that year. How much money will Terry have after 4 years?

6.4 Probability

1   With this spinner find the probability of getting:

(a) a 5   (b) a multiple of 4

(c) a prime number   (d) not an even number?

2 The probability of Sid's dog barking sometime in the morning is 0.97. What is the probability of Sid's dog not barking sometime in the morning?

3 A dice is thrown. What is the probability of getting:

(a) a 3   (b) a number less than 5   (c) a square number?

4

One card is chosen from above at random. Find the probability of getting:

(a) an 'S'   (b) not a 'T'   (C) a vowel

5 47% of the children in Year 8 in Colne Community School are boys. When Year 8 walk into an assembly, what is the probability that the first child to arrive will be a girl?

6 $\pi = 3.14159926$

One digit is chosen at random from the digits shown above. What is the probability of selecting:

(a) the digit '1'   (b) a digit which is not a prime number?

7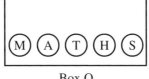

Box P   Box Q

Two boxes contain discs as shown.

(a) One disc is removed from box P. What is the probability of selecting a vowel? The disc is placed back in box P.

(b) Four more discs, (V) (E) (R) (Y), are added to box P. If one disc is now removed from box P, what is the probability of selecting a vowel? The disc is placed back in box P.

(c) The disc (A) is now taken out of box Q and placed in box P. If one disc is now removed from box P, what is the probability of selecting a vowel?

8 (a) Colin has a box with Mars bars and Milky Way bars inside it. If a bar is taken at random from the box, the probability of picking a Mars bar is $\frac{5}{7}$. What is the probability of picking a Milky Way?

(b) How many Mars Bars could there be in Colin's box to start with?

(c) Write down another two possibilities for the number of Mars bars that might be in Colin's box to start with.

9

| S | U | R | E | W | A | Y |

This old supermarket sign is in bad repair. One of the letters drops off.

(a) What is the probability that a vowel drops off.

(b) The letter 'E' drops off. If another letter drops off, what is the probability that it will be a vowel?

HWK 1E ————————————————————— **Main Book Page 330**

1 A bag contains yellow and red balls as shown. One ball is selected at random from the bag and then replaced. This is done 420 times. How many times would you expect to select:

(a) a red ball   (b) a yellow ball?

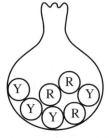

2 A fair dice is rolled 390 times. How many times would you expect to roll a multiple of 3?

3 The probability of it raining on any one day at Carnwell beach is $\frac{1}{3}$. On how many days would you expect it *not* to rain during a 3 week holiday at Carnwell beach?

4

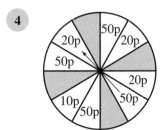

At a school fete a person pays 30p to spin the pointer opposite. The person will win the amount shown by the pointer. The game is played 480 times. What profit would the school expect to make?

5

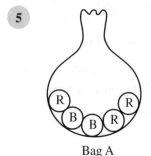

Bag A

Two bags have red (R) and black (B) balls in them as shown.

(a) Find the probability of selecting a black ball from bag A.

(b) A black ball is taken from bag A and put into bag B. A ball is then selected at random from bag B. What is the probability that this ball is not a black ball?

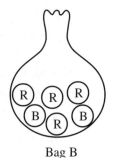

Bag B

6 Two out of every nine trains are late at Henton station. How many trains would you expect to be on time out of the next 54 trains to arrive at Henton station?

7 A coin is biased so that the probability of throwing 'tails' is 0.63. How many 'heads' would you expect when the coin is thrown 500 times?

8 Will has the Jack, Queen, King, Ace of Clubs and the Ace of Hearts. Amy chooses one of his cards and then Mark chooses one of his cards.

(a) If Amy chooses an Ace, what is the probability of Mark choosing an Ace?

(b) If Amy chooses a King, what is the probability of Mark choosing an Ace?

9 A bag contains n beads of which 7 are red. m beads are removed of which 2 are red. If one more bead is removed, what is the probability that it will be a red bead?

10 The probability of picking the winner of a horse race is p (p is a fraction). How many winners would you expect to pick for the next 45 races?

HWK 2M/2E ──────────────────────────────────── **Main Book Page 333**

1 (a) Ellie throws a coin and a dice. She could get a 'head' and a '5' (H 5). She could get a 'tail' and a '5' (T 5). List the 12 possible outcomes.

(b) What is the probability that Ellie would get a 'tail' and an odd number?

2 (a) Mindy uses a spinner (with the numbers 1, 2 and 3 on it) and a dice.

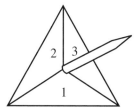 

She could get a '2' with the spinner and a '4' with the dice (2, 4).
She could get a '2' with the spinner and a '5' with the dice (2, 5).
List the 18 possible outcomes.

(b) What is the probability that she will get an odd number with both the spinner and the dice?

3 (a) Two dice are thrown. List all possible outcomes (there are 36 ways!) Copy and complete:

(1, 1) (2, 1) (3, 1) (4, 1) (5, 1) (6, 1)

(1, 2) (2, 2) (3, 2)   . . .   .

(1, 3)   . . .   .

 . . .   .

(b) What is the probability of throwing the same number on each dice?

4 A mother has 3 children. List all the possible outcomes to show if each child is a boy or a girl. Assuming that the probability of having a boy is $\frac{1}{2}$, what is the probability of the mother having:

(a) 3 boys   (b) exactly one girl?

5 A mother has 4 children. Assume that the probability of having a boy is $\frac{1}{2}$. By listing all the possible outcomes, find the probability of the mother having:

(a) 4 girls   (b) exactly one boy   (c) exactly two girls

HWK 3M ——————————————————————— **Main Book Page 336**

1 A bag contained some discs. Each disc has one of three letters on it – 'T', 'R' or 'Y'. Jan randomly takes a disc from the bag and then replaces it. She does this 80 times and records the results.

Letter	T	R	Y
Frequency	23	34	23

Estimate the probability that the next disc she takes out will be

(a) a 'Y'   (b) an 'R'

2 Lara rolls a fair dice 120 times. Each time she records the number it lands on.

Number	1	2	3	4	5	6
Frequency	22	25	4	23	27	19

(a) What seems 'strange' about these results?

(b) How many times would you have expected the dice to land on each different number?

(c) If Lara rolled the dice another 120 times, would you expect her to get the same results?

3 Chad and Marie throw a shoe to see if it will land on its heel or not. Chad throws 50 times and Marie throws 130 times. The results are shown below.

Chad

Throws	50
Heel landings	28

Marie

Throws	130
Heel landings	57

The shoe is thrown again.

(a) For Chad, what is the probability of the shoe landing on its heel?

(b) For Marie, what is the probability of the shoe landing on its heel?

(c) If you put Chad's and Marie's results together, what is the probability of the shoe landing on its heel if it is thrown again?

4 Toss a coin 50 times. How many tails would you expect to get?

Write down how your results compare to what you expected to get.

It you toss the coin another 50 times, would you expect to get the same result?

6.5 Drawing three dimensional objects

HWK 2M ———————————————————— **Main Book Page 342**

In questions **1** to **4** draw the plan view, the front view and the side view of the object.

1
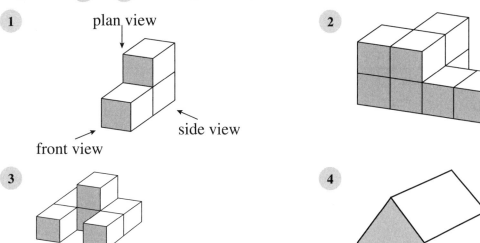
plan view

side view

front view

2

3

4

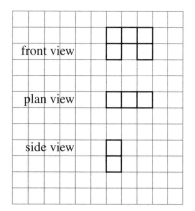
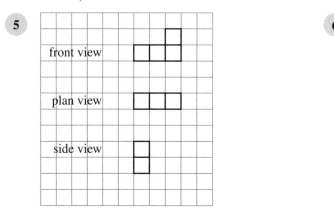

In questions **5** to **10** you are given three views of a shape. Draw each 3-D object (like those shown above).

5 front view

plan view

side view

6 front view

plan view

side view

7

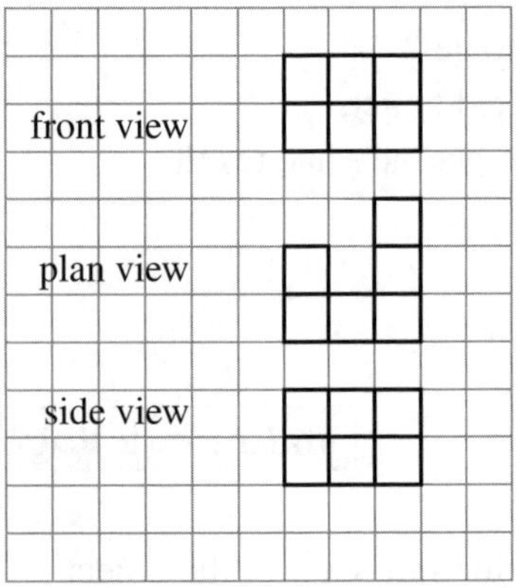

front view

plan view

side view

8

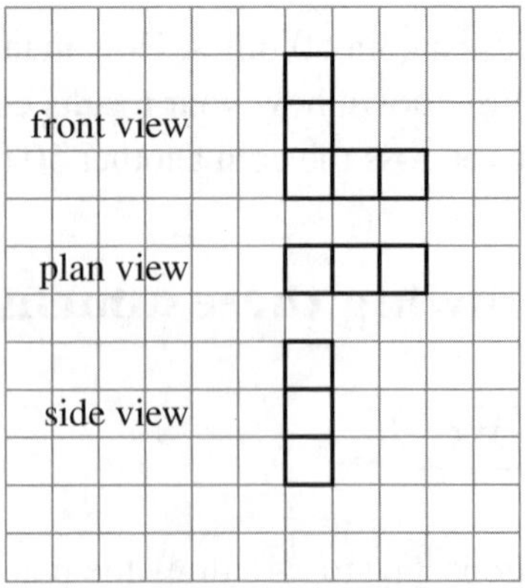

front view

plan view

side view

9

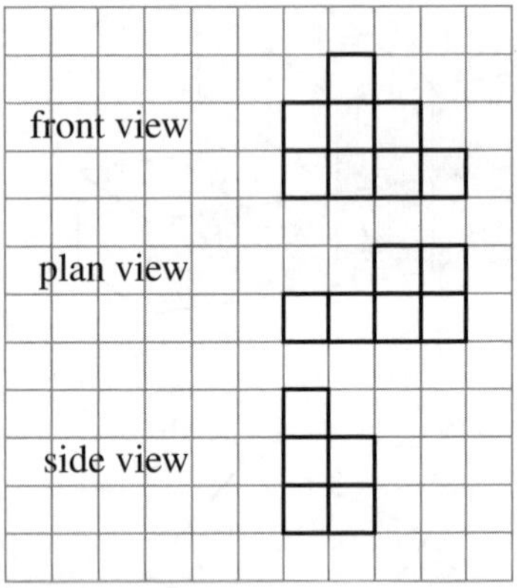

front view

plan view

side view

10

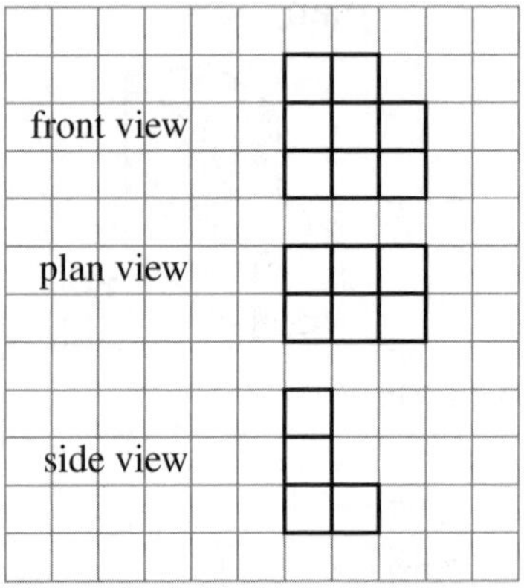

front view

plan view

side view